Sacred Body Wisdom

Mystical Conversations
Between Body & Spirit

By Michele Geyer

Photographs by Michele Geyer
Sacred Body Card Images & Cover Design by Melanie Pahlmann

Sacred Body Oracle & Cards™
The Energetic Connection, LLC
Olympia, WA

Sacred Body Wisdom & Sacred Body Cards
Copyright © 2013 by the Energetic Connection, LLC;
and Sacred Body Cards™
Third Edition Copyright © 2021

Sacred Body Cards:
ISBN# 978-0-9912521-1-4
Sacred Body Wisdom:
ISBN# 978-0-9912521-0-7

All rights reserved, including the right to reproduce this book or portions thereof in any form whatsoever. Scanning, printing, copying, in any way uploading and electronic sharing of any part of this book without the permission of the author is unlawful piracy and theft of the author's intellectual property.

Please See Terms of Use:
www.sacredbodypathworking.com/terms-of-use.html

If you would like to use material from the book (other than for review purposes) you must obtain prior written permission at the address provided here:
www.sacredbodypathworking.com/contact.html

Printed in the United States of America

Table of Contents

Preface	1
Introduction	6
Using the Cards	12
Maps & Spreads	22
Glossary of Terms	34

The Sacred Body Cards

Unity—Triquetra — 41

Organic Body—Vitruvian Man — 45
    Respiration-Air
    Digestion-Fire
    Circulation-Water
    Restoration-Earth
    Communication-Ether

The Elements—Pentacle — 59
    Eastern Wind
    Southern Sun
    Western Sea
    Northern Cave
    As Above, So Below

Sacred Cisterns—The Rose — 73
    Physical Body
    Etheric Body

Sacred Body Wisdom

    Astral Body
    Mental Body
    Spiritual Body
    Lower World
    Middle World
    Upper World

Rivers-Streams—Sacred Spiral   93
    Vital Vessels
    Sources76ff
    Anchorage
    The Riverbed
    Tributaries
    Streams
    Wellsprings
    Pools of Energy

Soul to Soul—Flower of Life   113
    Connection
    Origins
    Clear Sight
    Expressions
    Envisioning
    Consciousness
    Impressions
    Balance
    Knowingness
    Telepathy
    The Witness
    Record Keeper
    Healing

Sacred Body Wisdom

The Mystical Journey—Hermetic Qabala   144
    Strength
    Compassion
    Brilliance
    Evolution
    Vitality
    Expansion
    Intelligence
    Wisdom

Windows to the Soul—Wheel of Life   165
    Breath of Life
    Visualization
    Running Energy
    Inner Rhythms
    Cultivating Creativity
    Self-Inquiry & Reflection
    Awakening Awareness
    Self-Healing & Mastery

Gateways—Triple Spiral   185
    Body Currents
    Earth & Cosmic Energies
    Vortexes
    Primordial Power
    Life Forces
    Divine Matrix
    Creative Energy
    Spiritual Essence

Biographical Information   206
References   208

Gratitudes

My Creative Team:

Bill Georgevich & Melanie Pahlmann
Lucid Design Studios
Without whom, this oracle deck & cards would still be hiding in my inner cave!

Visionary of The Maps:

Ray Ristorcelli

My Personal Practice Partners:

Nancy Ondov & Timmi Montoya
For their commitment to personal growth & the evolution of our souls

Supportive Friends:

Patricia Everheart, Sandra Witbeck, Audrey Shannon, Mahara Daniel, Cathi Yamamoto, Amy Borel

My Teachers 1988-2020:

The many teachers at Berkeley Psychic Institute & Aesclepion Healing Center

Magic Isle: Lisa French & Staff

Sacred Body Wisdom

Body & Brain: Master Sylvia, Master HongIk, Master Oceana

The Skylonda Retreat Visionary Team & Original Staff

Alive & Well: Jocelyn Olivier, David Weinstock, Howard Nemerov

Pilates: Michele Larson & Joan Breibart; Celia Hulton, Ruth Alpert, Ray Kurshalls

Spiritual Teachers & Coaches: Lisa French, Sandra Kovacs, Laura Bruno

For their provocations while exploring my inner world and the body as sacred; for giving me the freedom to create, express & facilitate their work; which guided me to find, create and ultimately immerse myself in the evolution of my own work.

Preface

This is a book about self-awareness & reflection, practice & transformation.

I've come to realize and embrace the energetic *blueprint* (also referred to as the etheric body) as key in our physical healing. It took some time to fully embody this because it's so easy to fall back into a power-give-away and allow physical medicine—alternative or conventional—to rule choice.

From here on we will refer to the blueprint and the etheric body as one in the same. They are part of a subtle body network which includes several other subtle bodies, and shares the subtle anatomical parts known as the chakras, energy channels or nadis, and meridians among other parts.

After years of working with the physical body, years working with the subtle body network, and some more years working with both, I've finally come home to my personal ground zero.

And though it's important to eat healthy foods, cleanse regularly, express ourselves creatively and remain physically active, even more important is the balancing of our *etheric body and its blueprint* to restore and maintain our constitutional vitality. In fact, without that, our physical bodies can become diseased rather quickly and our vital energies depleted. Our physical healing needs to incorporate the full *subtle body network with special emphasis on the blueprint in the etheric body.*

Sacred Body Wisdom

Now that I have reached and surpassed the 60th year marker, I have personal experience with the potential for emptying this vitality bank account. Two years ago the stress of the previous years settled in, and my body decided to show me all the symptoms of dis-ease I'd accumulated over my lifetime which was exacerbated by more recent stresses.

Bear in mind that my lifestyle since I was a small child has been mostly, consciously healthy: primarily organic and vegan, lots of exercise, nature, outdoor activities, daily relaxation and meditation, self-reflection and emotional clearing. Of course I also had some "alternative fun."

What happened? Stress is what happened! Unresolved stress that began as an infant, imprinting and influencing my life experience on an endocrine, digestive, immune, and autonomic nervous system level in late adulthood. These physical-physiological responses can be directly translated into energetic and spiritual imbalances.

The miasms (disease encodement) stored in my *blueprint* downloaded into the physical body.

We come into this world with both energy savings and checking accounts. Throughout life we regularly deposit into, and withdraw resources from the checking account at various intervals: daily, monthly, etc., in the form of food, breath, rest, enjoyment and outputs that are often geared for stress management.

Now and then we create an overdraft and pull energy out of the savings to cover it. Sometimes we make a deposit, giving the savings account some extra padding, though not often because our world is so filed with stresses that drain both accounts of rejuvenating activities and their benefits. Top that with poor nutrient absorption and we have very little left over at the end of each paycheck to enhance our savings. So, we continue to live paycheck to paycheck, with a small savings for a rainy day.

As we reach 60—for some it shows up earlier or later, we begin to see more dramatically the aging effect, and the rapid depletion of both accounts, especially if we've lived a stressful life. Even at retirement age, we can still take home a regular paycheck, though it could be more challenging to keep up with the daily demands. This income is almost always dispersed solely into the checking account, and the checks and balances are usually tipped toward a higher outgo.

So, what happens? Our needs are not met by the checking account alone, so we dip further into the savings.

To keep up with the rate of depletion, we need to seriously reduce stress and add-in daily energy restoration practices like sleep, relaxation, gentle movement, energy gathering and circulation, and a quiet mind.

These practices are centered around healing our *etheric body* and the *blueprint codes*. In simple terms, all we need do is call-in the divine: earth and cosmos, and run that energy through us every day to both nourish and clear our *subtle body anatomy*. Even more to the point, spiritual life becomes the focus.

Sacred Body Wisdom

Here's a similar but different example of how the *etheric body blueprint* plays a role in our health.

Some years ago, I sat next to an energy healer at a networking lunch in my town. She was incredibly enthusiastic about her work as she told the group about her personal healing crisis and resultant return to health. According to this woman who looked bright and strong, her new discovery brought her back from multiple organ failure, and she was beginning to teach others to do the same work.

In the middle of the 90-minute lunch, I began to feel a strange pulling in my liver and a spiky sensation on my right side. Normally a big eater, I had trouble finishing my food that day. During the remainder of the lunch, I began to feel these same spiky-pulls in my intestines and stomach. I sat and listened, breathing deeply to relax the discomfort I felt in my body.

Afterwards, I cancelled the rest of my business day and went home to my couch. Organ by organ, I began to feel the same sensations in my kidneys and heart, my spleen and pancreas. By evening, every part of my body, including my bones and skin had experienced that same pulling sensation and sharpness. Very slowly again, the feelings disappeared, organ by organ.

Following that experience and some reflection, I eventually received some answers. A flash of communication came through about three days later. *"She may have healed her body, but her subtle body was still sick. She'd pushed the disease out of her physical awareness and downloaded the energy of her sickness into her blueprint."*

Sacred Body Wisdom

That was 2011.

I immediately began working with people to see, clear, experience and strengthen the *etheric body and blueprint.*

Many people have chronic health concerns that mysteriously come and go—much like the cancer patient who is treated and goes into remission, then reverts to ill health, and inevitably dies some day down the road from the disease.

Depending upon health and well-being on all levels, most continue to be baffled about why they never really heal, no matter how much energy, effort and supplements or medication they put into their physical health and spiritual practices.

I've had personal experience with this recently.

And like the energy healer I met that day at lunch who didn't quite finish her work because she forgot or didn't know how to get into the depths of clearing her *blueprint*, everyone's health issues and concerns need to be addressed and supported by clearing the physical and subtle bodies.

If I didn't know this when I first started working with energy over 30 years ago, I certainly know now, without a doubt, that working with the *blueprint* is paramount to fully heal any physical ailment as well as its emotional, mental and spiritual companions, which are part of the *subtle body network.*

Introduction

This is a journey through your inner terrain. The *Sacred Body Cards* are your guides. They symbolize and encourage the mystical conversation between body and spirit: the various ways that you speak to your body, the ways you are capable of enhancing your awareness of the subtle, spiritual forces moving through you, and the way your body and soul speak to one another. Rather than deny it, this awareness enhances your physical form. It's about integration—increasing your awareness of how your subtle and physical bodies are woven together, to heal both.

Mystical Metaphors

They express symbolism from several mystical traditions: Taoism, Yoga, Celtic Spirituality, Qabala, and Mystical Christianity. Rather than thinking of it as mixed and disparate metaphors, you might consider the possibility that all mystical traditions originate from the same source, and value similar qualities or virtues: honesty, kindness, grace, acceptance, truth, wisdom, self-knowledge, selflessness, no-thing-ness and non-dualism just to name some, all of which invite us to experience a direct link to the divine—the earth and cosmos within.

I like the Taoist Yin-Yang symbol to elucidate the way I see this truth:

Two black and white halves of equal size and shape exist within a circle. Each half contains the seed of the other. I see it as the *blueprint* for everything.

Sacred Body Wisdom

What is the Subtle Body?

In essence, the *subtle body network* is an energetic template that holds the energetic aspects of your physiological systems. You might see them as frequencies of vibration, sound and light.

More specifically, the subtle body contains the spiritual anatomy: meridians, nadis, chakras and polarity lines, as they are related to gross anatomy: circulatory, nervous and endocrine systems. In this book, we will use a simple model linking the physical to subtle body, the auric field and the chakras.

The physical body is essentially a denser hologram of the *subtle body network*. Like the spinal column in the physical body, the *blueprint* also has a centerline or central channel. Instead of a spinal cord, cerebral spinal fluid and nerve-blood plexi, the subtle body has chakras, chi or kundalini in the central channel, and subtle channels that reach out from the chakras into the rest of the *subtle body network* just like nerves and arteries reach into the periphery of your physical body. Rather than overlays or an underlayment, each subtle body is woven into and through our human form.

The *blueprint—expressed in the etheric body*, holds miasms (underlying disease patterns—with genetic, morphogenetic and environmental origins), and the encodement for health. When a miasm is awakened it affects all levels of existence: physical, mental, emotional and spiritual. A dichotomy exists, as it is both cause and effect.

In addition, we could say the physical body is formed from the *blueprint* inside the *etheric body*, within the *subtle body network*. Healing the *blueprint* heals the *etheric body* which propels us further in our evolution. This healing could be seen as the fuel that propels us through the gateway into higher levels.

The Intention of the Cards

This is an oracle deck of awareness and practices, designed to help you connect your physical body to spirit through the *blueprint*, awakening and remembering the divine within you.

Each section or *Sacred Gateway* theme calls attention to where you are on the path of personal evolution at particular points in time and space, as related to your current inquiry, whether that is with the guidance of one card, or includes a whole spread. Follow the different maps, pull the cards, refer to the book and interpret for yourself. This will guide or remind you how to transform knowledge to wisdom through practice, every day choices, and actions.

Your journey can potentially begin at any point along the way, wherever you are in present time. With focus and intention, you can simply walk through the door that is open to you. Whether self-directed or in a pre-determined spread, each card and its position will offer information related to your inquiry and intention.

Generally speaking, in any given moment, your conscious journey can begin in the physical body—from a thought, sensation, or emotion. At another time, your journey might begin with a spiritual experience. No matter what the catalyst or opening, you will always find what you need and take whatever steps are necessary before completing and returning to center, wherever that may be here and now.

Stay curious.

Remember as you wander, you can apply any of the symbolism in the physical and spiritual realms or both. Always look for the energetic links and reflections in any card you encounter, and consider the metaphors as the keys to your discovery.

Sacred Body Oracle and Cards are about potential—your human potential to know yourself, to heal, grow and make changes; to transmit—simply by being, your wholeness, your divinity, your humanity and your affinity for yourself and others.

This deck is designed to be inspirational and provocative; to help you evoke from within—self-inquiry and reflection, self-healing and mastery. Rather than answers, each card will ask you to consider new questions that will guide you down a path of self-discovery, through curiosity and discipline. You will evoke much from your unexplored inner terrain.

The Sacred Gates: Basic Theme Information

Each of the 9 themes in the *Sacred Body Cards* is a *Sacred Gateway* to another level of consciousness and self-awareness, each with a series of internal *Stepping Stones* that take you to the next *Sacred Gateway*. Your path may take you in an orderly fashion up through the steps, or you may want to experience a more spontaneous and winding route through these mountains and valleys.

Unity is at center, potentially symbolizing the beginning and the end of your journey. It is the only card in its theme.

The *Organic Body* theme begins at birth and your evolving relationship with your physical form. There are 6 cards in this theme.

The Elements weave the physical and subtle bodies together, symbolizing the links to and communication between the physical and the energetic, the planet, humanity, and all beings. There are 6 cards in this theme.

Sacred Cisterns are metaphors for the subtle body centerline: the links between the aura, the chakras and the secondary subtle bodies. In the mystical Qabalistic tradition, these cisterns are represented by the middle road on the journey. There are 9 cards in this theme.

Rivers & Streams represent the energy centers and channels of the subtle body. There are 9 cards in this theme.

Soul to Soul represents the human capacity for subtle, psychic communication. There are 14 cards in this theme.

Sacred Body Wisdom

The Mystical Journey symbolizes the choices you must make for advancement along the path inside your journey. There are 9 cards in this theme.

Windows to the Soul are practices that increase your awareness and take you beyond the glass ceiling of potential, into the realms of wisdom through awareness and consciousness. There are 9 cards in this theme.

Gateways to the Heights are the energies that flow through your subtle body. There are 9 cards in this theme.

The Mystic's Journey: Stepping Stones Between the Sacred Gates

Inside the framework of each theme *(Sacred Gateways)* are the smaller benchmarks, or *Stepping Stones* on the journey. There are between 5 and 13 *Stepping Stones* in each theme, between the *Sacred Gateways*.

Using the Sacred Body Cards

The Simplest Way

Single Card: Pull a card, reflect on its imagery and symbolism, find its page and read about the details of that card, and its related theme information.

Daily Sequence: Arrange the 72 cards in order: from *Organic Body* to *Unity* (use the table of contents as a list), and then follow a daily sequence of discovery through the cards for 72 days, hours or weeks—any timetable you choose.

Let's keep the symbolism as simple as possible for now. The companion book will give you hints that will provoke your curiosity and your consciousness, leaving the depth of these cards—their potential and applications of the information, for your personal exploration and inner truth.

The Next Level: Common Threads

Divining as your personal adventure: Familiarize yourself with the basics and learn about some of the landmarks you might encounter on your journey. It's always a great idea to pull individual cards for a while and familiarize yourself with the images, symbols and descriptions. Once you are ready, you can take the next step into path-working, maps and more complex spreads. Here's a little information about the symbolism.

Sacred Body Wisdom

Organizing your Cards: First, put aside the *Unity* card—one of 9 *Sacred Gateway* (theme) cards. In a moment you'll use it as a sample guide for all the other theme cards.

Lay out your deck of 72 cards in the order found in the table of contents, beginning with *Organic Body*—another *Sacred Gateway* card. You can lay out all the cards theme by theme, row by row, to see the bigger picture if you like.

Second, using the table of contents, and beginning with *the Organic Body*, notice how each of the nine *Sacred Gateway* cards sets a tone for their specific theme of 6-14 cards. These foundational theme pages for each *Sacred Gateway* are identified in bold under the *Sacred Body Cards* section of the table of contents. They offer general information about each theme which pertains to all cards in that particular theme.

Observing the big picture with all your cards laid out in rows and columns, according to their themes, will show you a bit more about how they are organized in terms of personal growth, your soul's purpose and evolution.

Primary Images & Symbols: Let's bring back the *Unity* card now and look closely at its symbols and images. We'll use it here as a sample for the other *Sacred Gateways* as well.

There is one primary photographic image—Redwood trees in this sense, and a theme-related sacred symbol in the lower center of each *Sacred Gateway* card.

Sacred Body Wisdom

The *Celtic Triquetra,* lies at the bottom center of the *Unity* card. Different sacred symbols are used for each theme and are displayed in the same location on all the cards—lower center.

Another example is the *Vitruvian Man* in the bottom center of the *Organic Body* theme card. This sacred symbol links together all cards in its theme.

As you begin to use the cards, you'll become more aware and accustomed to their common threads. For now, simply look at each suit to see the similarities between the cards and how their individual symbolism is expressed.

Just remember, the key components of the cards are: the primary image, and the symbol at bottom center. Next we'll take a look at the symbols in the right margin and the thumbnail images in the upper left corner of the Stepping Stone cards.

Secondary Symbols: Notice the right margin symbols on all cards, and a thumbnail image in the upper left corner of each *Stepping Stone* card.

These are the secondary symbols for each theme. The *Organic Body* theme is directly linked to 5 themes as indicated in the right margin symbolism—all cards in its own theme and 4 others. Some themes are linked to all 9 themes; some are linked to many fewer themes. The symbols in the right hand margin will inform you about these connections.

The thumbnail images in the upper left corner of each *Organic*

Body Stepping Stone card represent the elemental symbols for alchemy, and speak to its individuality, as well as its theme connections. All *Organic Body* cards have an elemental alchemy symbol. Other suits will display unique thumbnail images symbolizing different types of connections to their theme partners.

Card Description Pages: Each *Sacred Gateway* and related theme card has its own page of descriptions, provocations and symbolism, as do all the *Stepping Stones* cards. Within that symbolism, other cards are identified as related to the card you have pulled. These relations are identified in bold under the "Your Blueprint" section.

Once you begin pulling cards and using the spreads, you'll notice that many connections are left undefined in this book of symbols. Rather than an omission, the purpose here is to encourage you to explore, learn and grow by studying the cards, their images and sacred symbolism, the primary and secondary connections between the cards.

To use this manual, you must be imaginative and willing to explore! Use the cards in their own pre-scribed evolutionary path from *Unity* through the 9 *Sacred Gateways*, or you can pull random cards with intention, placing them in all the pre-scribed locations within the spreads.

Use the maps provided, or create your own paths.

Try pulling a card a day for a while, spending some time reflecting on the images and symbols. What do they suggest to you; what do they elicit from you?

Practices

There are suggested practices written into the pages for each *Stepping Stone* card and questions posed for self-reflection. Similarly, yet with a deeper understanding and commitment, the *Windows to the Soul* theme is the *Sacred Gateway* where knowledge becomes wisdom through various disciplines or practices. There are 8 windows and 8 types of practice: *Breath, Visualization, Energy Awareness, Movement, Energy Circulation, Self-Reflection, Witnessing, and Self- Mastery.* Some practices may seem to be repeats of the same, though they are actually building blocks that trigger deeper experiences using similar tools. Each practice builds upon the next, yet can be performed in any order, at any time as well.

Although quite gentle, some of the movement practices may contraindicated for your personal condition. Please move only in a range that is comfortable for your body, and always consult with your health care professional before attempting any new exercise.

Things to keep in mind when practicing:
1. Be gentle with yourself, aware of your current state of mind and body.

2. If you are uncertain about a specific practice, consult your inner guidance or your health care professional to see if it is appropriate for your current state of health and well-being.

3. The suggested practices are safe if done thoughtfully, slowly

and in a comfortable range of motion, yet some of the physical exercises may be contraindicated for certain conditions. Please check with your health care provider before you attempt any new exercises. None of them are intended to replace needed medical attention.

4. Repeat each exercise 3x, 6x, or 9x. As you advance, build repetition in the same increments.

5. Practice assists you in becoming aware of yourself in deeper ways by anchoring your energy in your body and taking ownership of your personal space.

6. Not all practices suggested are designed to be solely meditative. If you were to walk the path of the cards in the order of their prescribed evolution, you would practice in relation to that order by:

Sensing: Organic Body, The Elements
Feeling: Sacred Cisterns, Rivers & Streams
Visualizing: Soul to Soul, Windows to the Soul
Experiencing: The Mystical Journey, Gateways to the Heights
Being: Unity

7. A more detailed version of each practice is available. Check our *Sacred Body Wisdom* blog: sacredbodywisdom.com; or our website: sacredbodyoracleandcards.com, for the launch of our next companion books, *"Relax Your Body, Quiet Your Mind: 52 Ways to Relieve Stress & Go Within;"* and the *"Sacred Body Calendar Journal."*

Some of the more common and self-induced *meditative practices* include:

Passive/Receptive: Taking time for *conscious relaxation and inner exploration.*

-Sitting in stillness, *quiet time,* waiting, allowing images or relaxed states to appear.

-Listening to scripted or *guided visualization* and instruction; relaxing music or sounds.

-Restorative Yoga supports and assists the body in reaching a relaxed state—thoughts recede and the mind becomes quiet.

-Yoga Nidra, also known as yoga sleep, takes you down through the levels of physical, mental and emotional relaxation, until you reach the bridge between alpha and theta brainwaves.

Active/Creative: exploring the imaginal by *creating specific images.*

-Singular Focus: *holding an image* or sacred symbol in your mind's eye.

-Guided Visualization: use of *mental imagery* to relax or explore the inner realms; can also be self-directed.

-Conscious Breathing: can be a simple awareness practice that follows the path of the breath; or it might encourage you to create various breathing patterns with specific instructions.

Sacred Body Wisdom

-Inquiry: *thinking or reflecting* about the meaning of something; speaking with oneself through the inner voice.

Path-working

There are many ways to use the *Sacred Body Cards* as a map for specific and directed path-working: an evolutionary series of symbols, metaphors, images, reflections and practices for self-improvement and inner growth.

Path-working is often a pre-scribed path, yet it is unnecessary to follow any but your own route and inner guidance. As mentioned earlier, you may begin with our maps and spreads, which are outlined in these pages, using the cards in their own evolutionary order, or feel free to shuffle, cut and pull cards from your stack to see where you are spontaneously directed or called. Sometimes the maps remain the same yet the landmarks are different.

As you read on, you'll find there are common threads between path-working, maps and spreads. They are identified by the same names. Consult the section on *The Maps* for more information.

A Basic Linear Path: 72 Cards explored over 72 Days and or in 72 evolutionary steps. Shuffle and pull randomly or use them in order.

The Sacred Spiral: moving outward from *Unity* into the *Organic Body* and inward from birth back to *Unity*, using all 72 cards in order, or pulling randomly.

The Wheel of Life: a seasonal approach to growth that is anchored in the center at *Unity*. It begins with the *Organic Body* theme at Imbolc-Candelmas in the beginning of February, and ends with *Gateways to the Heights* during Winter Solstice-Yuletide. This path is best expressed by laying out the 9 *Sacred Gateways* theme cards in their order, and then randomly pulling the remaining cards as the *Stepping Stones* cards in between for a deeper inquiries into each season.

Through the Wisdom Rings: Your journey is focused on 9 rings of wisdom symbolized by the 9 *Sacred Gateways* themes, beginning with the *Organic Body* and relatively unconscious realms, through the evolutionary stages of growth, ultimately moving into full consciousness at *Unity*. This path is best expressed by using the *Sacred Gateways* cards in their order, then shuffling and randomly pulling the remaining cards as the *Stepping Stones* in between.

Advancing through the levels of consciousness includes explorations and actions in each ring of wisdom:

1. Habits & Comfort Zone
2. Making New Choices
3. Focus & Goals
4. Discernment: Hope or Intention
5. Expression, Support & Service
6. Moving Beyond Your Insights
7. True Interactivity & Self Trust
8. Sustaining Higher Vibrations
9. Amusement & Enthusiasm

Sacred Body Wisdom

Triple Spiral: The focus of your journey here is to create balance and integrity in successive realms of land, sea and sky. As you complete in one realm, its energy forms a spiraling wave that carries you into the next realm. There are 3 levels within each realm. It is best to find spontaneity here, allowing the cards to express randomly.

Six-Pointed Star: As above, so below. Heaven seeks Earth and Earth opens to Heaven in this Divine Embrace. Your journey will expose how open your body is to spirit with randomly selected cards for best results.

Body to Spirit Communication

No matter what the avenue, its length, or the time you spend there, whether you take the guided, pre-scribed tour with the maps and spreads, or pull your own as you go, each step along the way engages you in a dialogue that has potential to move you beyond your current state of awareness to the next *Sacred Gateway*.

Coupled with sincere practice, you can open yourself to spirit in ways you've never experienced before, developing a very deep relationship with the divine inside. One of the most important goals, or better said, *intentions*, is to connect with the divine through the sources of earth and sky, increasing your communication with the god of your heart, developing a deep sense of self-affinity to compassionately witness life, interacting with all other beings.

Know Thyself. This is all that truly matters.

Maps & Spreads

The Maps

Each map offers many roads and possibilities as you move into and out of center. You can spiral through one step at a time, thoughtfully experiencing all states of your being-ness. You can take a short cut and walk through the rings of wisdom directly into center. You can circle around the edge of the wheel, visiting each season, element and direction, spontaneously dipping a toe in or diving deeply along the way, returning over and over again as you create and watch the ripples of your existence. And, you can bushwhack your own path!

Whatever the path or map, your prescribed journey begins in *Unity* at the threshold between lives. From this place, you choose how and where to make your entrance, scanning your soul, its past, its purpose, the times you are about to enter. You consider the possibilities, reflecting on your experience in the body this lifetime, and how that is best created or accomplished. After much inquiry, you begin your spiraling journey through the *Sacred Gateways* into the body.

Moving through the various stages of evolution and development, you exit through the portal between dimensions, the space between the cosmos and life on earth. While in the body you listen for your personal soul song and its messages as you write the script of your life. You make choices as you listen to your inner voice and the world around you, searching for the feeling of *Unity* you remember so very vividly, deep in your being. At times you struggle and in others you move with ease and great joy, always

Sacred Body Wisdom

searching for your truth, your contribution and finally, your way back home to *Unity*.

See the next section on *Spreads* on page 26 for more information about laying out the cards.

The Sacred Spiral: This route guides you on a methodical step-by-step process from birth to integration. The spiral moves in both directions, as the journey is cyclically informing all aspects of your being as a foundation for evolution. It all unfolds, step by step, symbol by symbol.

The Wheel of Life: This map takes you on an exploration around the outer edges of the *Wheel of Life* through the seasons and cycles of all kinds. You can choose to go deeper into each season, experiencing the elemental and other related energies by

moving toward center. The paths narrow, the learning curve gets steeper and growth becomes more concentrated, even intense, as you move into center. Journey through the void or draw on the cards for guidance, unfolding with each step you take inward.

Rings of Wisdom: Each of the 9 rings from the center to the outermost layer is related to a level of consciousness. Each level can be accessed by walking directly through each layer, or by spiraling in through the various *Sacred Gateways* and related *Stepping Stones*.

The Triple Spiral: The ancient Celts, especially from the Druidic path, see the triple spiral as a metaphor for land, sea and sky. We can take this a bit further and suggest its metaphor extends to: earth, human, and heaven; physical, emotional-mental, and spiritual; or even conscious, subconscious and unconscious realms. Whatever way you might see this triad, the triple spiral is like a wave that carries you from one realm to another. Each growth point washes you into the next realm; at first on the outer orbit of the spiral, going deeper, more inward as you evolve through each realm.

The Six Pointed Star: As above, so below, the six-pointed star has an ancient symbolism that goes beyond the religious: heaven merging with earth, masculine diving into feminine; spirit embodied. Consider the two triangles merging as the Universal principle of give and take or masculine and feminine: one receptive and one active component to create an integrated whole. One does not work without the other, and the two energies combined have a synergy that is not present with two separate pieces.

Sacred Body Wisdom

The Evolutionary Path: Energy of the Sacred Gates

There are 9 primary themes or *Sacred Gateways* in the Sacred Body Cards. All but the *Unity* theme contains 5-13 *Stepping Stones* within it. Each theme and related symbolism builds upon the next theme. There are many maps to one destination and many routes into center.

Organic Body: Birth, human physiology. Realization the body is organic, human.

The Elements: Subtle body, nature. Realization that the body is tied to natural law and the elements; early stages of recognition about the energetic nature of all things.

Sacred Cisterns: The first step onto the energetic path begins with an essential awareness about where energy meets physiology as a prelude to future experience. These are the energetic links to the subtle bodies, which exist as a mirror for the human body's spinal column, and emanate out into the aura. This central channel of energy is the source of all other energy channels and chakras that link to the subtler forms.

Rivers & Streams: Exploration of the subtle energy channels and subtle anatomy. Practical awareness skills enhance the depth of experience as subtle body awareness peaks.

Soul to Soul: Inner voice or subtle internal communication begins with the self, eventually expanding into relationships with others and the outer world. Awareness of your psychic capacity for creation and communication becomes known: it is inherent in the human brain.

Mystical Journey: Risk, trial and error, self- discovery, excavation of shadow material, duality, polarities, and dichotomies, all become known at this level; the beginnings of "walking the talk" on the road to enlightenment.

Windows to the Soul: Awareness assists in body-spirit integration through discipline and ultimately recognition that regular, active practice is needed to sustain and progress. Sincere, devotional practices hold the imprint of the *Wheel of Life,* and the seeds of Universal and possibly eternal evolution.

Gateways to the Heights: Recognition of the subtle energies that move through you and a state of divine energy revelation.

Unity: At center lies your autonomy and sovereignty. It is the threshold, a place from which to view your eternal connection to all dimensions, past and future lives. A place of completion and integration, there are no polarities here. Your ability to be conscious of your unconscious capabilities and awareness of awareness exist here.

The Spreads

Most of the spreads here are based on *Path-working* and *The Maps* you just read about. Each one is uniquely designed with the *Sacred Body Cards* and symbols in mind. The questions and statements found in these *Spreads* can be turned into instruction, a set of inquiries, positive reflection, and potential information for self-confrontation. It really depends upon what you are willing to see and learn about yourself in any given moment.

All *Sacred Body Cards* are positive, there are no reversed meanings, though they reflect the inherent dynamics and the dichotomy of a spiritual life in the body. You can discern their shadow potential as you read the cards and reflect on how each one relates to your inquiry and the overall map or spread you've chosen. Each card represents conscious and unconscious support, reflection, internal filters and constructs, and many other considerations for you.

You may want to create templates for your favorite spreads using poster board and art supplies so you can place the cards in their proper positions as you move through the unfolding messages of your inner oracle.

Before you begin: Light a candle, ground your body, anchor your energy in your body, breathe naturally until you feel your body relax and your mind becomes quiet.

Reaching an *Alpha Brainwave* state is important in accessing your inner or imaginal planes. The key is to move away from the daily stresses of narrow focus and rigid attention, into a broader state of relaxed consciousness. Most of the practices mentioned here will ultimately take you into that state. Even so, if you have trouble reaching a relaxed state, there are many pre-recorded CD's with sounds that will assist you: Hemi-Synch, Jeffrey Thompson's Brainwave Suite, Whole Tones, nature sounds, and more.

Sacred Body Wisdom

Once you get where you want to be, set your intention and focus on your inquiry as you shuffle, and then cut the deck three times. Now lay out the cards in one of the following spreads or in one of your own creations.

Single Card Inquiry

Pull one card anytime for a quick reflection of your growth. There are no yes and no answers. It's best to ask *how the divine sees you in present time; or, what is the most important information for you now; or, what do you need to interact with most.*

The Sacred Spiral—9 cards

From the human perspective, your existence is often seen in linear form, even in terms of eternity. Tribal cultures like the Celts and the Mayans created a circular or spiral calendar to symbolize time and the seasons. Lay out one card at a time, arranging your 9 cards in a loose spiral as you go. Overlap the corner of each card so your last card can horizontally bridge the gap between the beginning and ending. Use this spread as a creative cycle. What do you want to create?

Card 1: Who are you now in relation to your inquiry?

Card 2: What have you already created as a foundation for advancement?

Card 3: What do you need to clear before you move forward?

Card 4: What wisdom was hidden and is now present?

Card 5: What is key in your new plan?

Card 6: What is your next step in this creation?

Card 7: How can you best embrace your creation?

Card 8: What is your outcome?

Card 9: How can you bridge your present-time self with the outcome?

The Rings of Wisdom—10 cards

Use this spread as a symbol of the age or wisdom rings in the inner core of your personal tree of life. Each card represents a level of awareness or consciousness that you will pass through on your journey. Lay out the cards one by one as though they sit within the 9 concentric rings of your inner tree.

Card 1: The Core: Who are you now?

Card 2: First Ring (outermost): What is your comfort zone?

Card 3: Second Ring: What are you waiting for, what information do you need?

Card 4: Third Ring: What desires are in your way?

Card 5: Fourth Ring: How does hope stop your ability to create and receive?

Card 6: Fifth Ring: What will help you become more certain?

Card 7: Sixth Ring: How do your existing insights actually create instability and stagnancy along the way?

Card 8: Seventh Ring: What will help you to trust yourself?

Card 9: Eighth Ring: What more do you need to explore?

Card 10: Ninth Ring: The Outcome: What have you achieved, or where are you in your own evolution?

The Wheel of Life—10 cards

You can gauge your personal cycles by the Moon, the seasons, your creative process, or any other natural cycle. Use this spread to establish a path for a specific vision or interest, or to see more clearly one that is already in process. Place one card in center and then one-by-one arrange the next 8 cards in a circle around center according to the 8 seasons.

Card 1: Center: You in present time

Card 2: NE: Imbolc: Planting the Seeds

Card 3: East: Spring: Inspiration & New Beginnings

Sacred Body Wisdom

Card 4: SE: Beltane: Fertility, Abundance

Card 5: South: Mid-Summer: Cleansing & Transformation

Card 6: SW: Lughnasadh: Early Harvest

Card 7: West: Autumn Equinox: Harvest & Devotion

Card 8: NW: Samhain: Endings, Late Harvest

Card 9: North: Mid-winter: Restoration & Healing

Card 10: The Outcome of Your Intentions

The Divine Embrace: Six Pointed Star—8 cards

You are a receiving vessel for the divine which seeks earthly spaces to fill with its golden light. This spread connects heaven and earth through the body. Use it to see your truth in present time regarding specific situations and people in your life. Or, simply become the observer of where you are on your path. Begin by placing one card in the middle, then proceed to lay out the cards in the shape of a 6-pointed star, one card at each point. The eighth card will lay over the first card as you complete the spread.

Card 1 (in Center) *I AM: Soul*

Card 2 (lowest point of lower triangle): *Ground of Being:* what energy do you carry in present time and or what is the foundation for this situation? What are the resources you have funded for this scenario or circumstance?

Card 3 (Right point of lower triangle): *Release:* What needs to be released or surrendered so you can create space for and receive the abundance of the Divine?

Card 4 (Left point of lower triangle): *Hidden:* What is hidden from your view that needs to be unveiled or brought to consciousness? What is your unfinished business?

Card 5 (Left point of upper triangle): *Bridge:* What will help you bridge the gap or integrate your physical world with the Divine? How can you be more open to receiving?

Card 6 (Right point of upper triangle): *Embrace:* What qualities do you need to embrace in yourself to grow into your intention? What do you now hold that you can offer to the Divine?

Card 7 (Upper-most point of upper triangle): *Integrity:* How is your work integrated now? What is the next step on your spiritual path? How do you get there from here?

Card 8 (middle overlapping the first, *"I AM"* card): *Creation:* The last card represents the outcome or result of the steps you have taken or will soon take in relation to this spread. In other words, to where will you ascend when you commit to the wisdom of Divine Embrace? Place this card in the center, on top of *"I AM."*

Triple Spiral—4-13 cards

Here, you might ask for input on how the three realms (aspects) are currently influencing your life and how you can balance, integrate, or clear something if need be. You might do one level in each realm, or all 3 levels.

When looking into all 3 levels, you will use 12 cards plus an additional card for a look at potential outcome. Each card (#'s 1, 2, 3) represents one realm; each word assigned to the realms represents a level or layer within the realm.

Simply begin with three realms and three cards: one in each spiral realm. Follow by laying another card on top of each as you move through the layers—example: Land, Earth, Mother, Unconscious Energy & Body.

Card 1: Land, Unconscious Energy, Physical-Body

Card 2: Sea, Subconscious Energy, Emotional-Mind

Card 3: Sky, Conscious Energy, Psycho-Spiritual

The maps and spreads here have been created by the author. Although the symbols are sacred and universal and can be used by anyone, the actual spreads and maps are unique to the Sacred Body Oracle and Cards, and Sacred Body Wisdom. They are intellectual property, copyrighted and owned by the Energetic Connection, LLC.

Glossary of Terms

-*Afference*: energy that moves into center

-*Akashic Records:* eternal knowledge encoded on the spiritual planes available through psychic means

-*Apana*: downward moving energy, aids release of stagnancy—physically and energetically

-*Aura:* energy field, electromagnetic field

-*Awareness:* realization, perception, consciousness

-*Cauldrons:* three primary energy centers related to subtle bodies: lower abdomen, chest, and neck-head region

-*Central Channel:* centerline; also see pranic tube, shushumna

-*Chakras:* wheels of energy anchored in the subtle body central channel (blueprint), mirroring the spinal column and nerve plexi

-*Chi*: life force; also see prana

-*Cisterns:* cauldrons

-*Clairaudience:* ability to hear spirit

-Clairsentience: sympathy, ability to feel another's pain or physical sensation; differs from empathy

-Clairvoyance: clear sight, inner sight, psychic or soul sight, ability to see spirit

-Conscious: existing in a state of regular awareness; related to upper brain and frontal lobe; short-term memory

-Cosmic Energy: heavenly energy

-Dichotomy: two sides of the same coin or structure creating opposing parts

-Efference: energy moving away from center

-Empathy: ability to feel another's emotions; ability to interact from higher emotions

-Energy Field: electromagnetic field, aura

-Etheric Body: subtle body, esoteric body, the blueprint

-Flower of Life: sacred geometrical shape of multiple conjoined circles; contains the fundamentals of spiritual life

-Hologram for the Divine: all things great and small (mineral, plant, animal, human, angelic, unknown); from single cells to complex beings, everything holds imprints of the source

-Human Torus: self-perpetuating energy originating from within the pranic tube or central channel, circulating through the subtle and physical bodies, and into the auric field

-Ida: feminine energy line; parasympathetic branch of the autonomic nervous system; see also *Pingala*

-Inner Kingdom: sanctuary, center of head; pituitary, pineal, thalamus & hypothalamus glands; all link to the Big Dipper & the Polestar through the crown of the head; hypothalamus links directly to the endocrine & nervous systems

-Kundalini: liquid golden light, subtle body energy, potent life force, cerebral spinal fluid

-Lower World: World of rebirth and transformation; see Upper and Middle Worlds

-Meridians: longitudinal masculine and feminine energy lines and connections; subtly defined in the blueprint and fascia of the physical body and also in the energy field as related to the elements and the cosmos

-Middle World: human world and the world of nature spirits; see Lower and Upper Worlds

-Morphogenic (or morphogenetic) Fields: shared or common fields of energy

-Nadis: subtle energy channels in the body and energy field

-Pelvic Bowl: the lower abdomen

-Pelvic Floor: soft tissues between the four bony pelvic points: pubic, tail and sitting bones

-Pentacle: five-pointed star symbolizing the five elements

-Pingala: masculine energy line, sympathetic branch of the autonomic nervous system; see also *Ida*

-Polarity: magnetics, opposite energies

-Portals: a gateway, opening or doorway into another realm or dimension

-Prana: upward moving life force, nourishment

-Pranic tube: central channel; prana flows through it

-Pre-cognition: foresight, ability to know before something happens

-Psychometry: "seeing or sensing" through the hands

-Qabala: Tree of Life as adopted by Western Esotericism-Mysticism

-Rose: sacred flower symbolizing the depth of relationship, growth and spiritual essence

-Sacred Spiral: a singular spiral or vortex of energy

-*Shushumna:* central channel or pillar, pranic tube, central nervous system

-*Six-Pointed Star:* heaven embodied, As Above, So Below

-*Subconscious:* related to what lies underneath the conscious mind or thoughts; midbrain, emotions and bio-chemistry

-*Subtle Body:* the blueprint or etheric body; non-physical energy, vortexes and channels

-*Triple Spiral* (Celtic): three linked spirals symbolizing land, sea and sky; or body, mind-emotion and spirit

-*Triquetra:* sacred Celtic trinity symbol

-*Unconscious*: information that is stored, or repressed states of being, held in a state of non-regular awareness, unknown; lower brain

-*Upper World:* spirit world; see Lower & Middle Worlds

-*Vitruvian Man:* (DaVinci) proportional human form as connected to the elements and the cosmos

-*Wheel of Life*: seasonal wheel of cycles; directions, elements, and existence

The Sacred Body Cards

Unity

At the Threshold

Only from center where the garden of autonomy grows, can unity be truly experienced. Like the ardent Redwood, whose taproot is long and anchored deep, you have a singular connection into the earth, while the fingers of another system crawl just under the surface to all other redwoods. Its hearty trunk supports branches that reach to the heavens. Hand in hand, you too, exist in community.

Sacred Body Wisdom

Redwood Trees are self-perpetuating, yet always grow in relation to community. Some of the broadest and tallest trees in existence, they stand like sentries protecting the forests of the Sierra Nevada and along coastal highways in the Pacific Northwestern United States. These red giants thrive primarily in clean coastal air, deep in the mists of the fog belts near the western sea.

The Celtic Triquetra is a trinity symbol that bridges religion; spirituality; nature; the pagan Triple Goddess; upper, middle and lower worlds; the triune brain qualities: instinct, emotion & conscious intention; the three levels of creativity: procreation, manifestation, and divine co-creation.

Your Body: Much like the many metaphors of this symbolism—you are the tree of life, rooted in the lower world through your feet and legs; reaching to the upper world with your arms, neck and head, from the trunk or torso and all it contains, in the middle world. The *Unity* card encompasses all beings, all things.

Your Blueprint: In *Unity* we exist in a state of no time-no space, inside a place before the soul is linked with the body. The metaphorical Redwood tree is the hologram we fill and embody on Earth.

Nature : Redwood Tree, Elements, Mother, Gaia, Earth, Heaven, Sky, Cosmos, Spiritual or Universal Web of connection.

Energetic Connections: *Unity* links to all other *Sacred Body Cards* and sacred symbolism. For additional information, read about these symbols and *Sacred Gateways*:

Triquetra—Unity
Vitruvian Man—Organic Body
Pentacle—The Elements
Rose—Sacred Cisterns
Sacred Spiral—Rivers & Streams
Flower of Life—Soul to Soul
Qabala—Mystical Journey
Wheel of Life—Windows to the Soul
Triple Spiral—Gateways to the Heights

Your Map: Unity is at center—the place from which all journeys begin, and all journeys end. It is the womb that births us in the beginning, and collects us in the end. Unity is the place of full integration and in a human evolutionary sense it can symbolize individuation—whole or complete, yet separated from the beliefs ideas of the collective unconscious.

From Unity, we reflect on our past and contemplate our next incarnation, spiraling outward from the threshold between lives. We begin our descent as a soul, moving out into the physical world, through our life experiences and back into center again. Like Dante's Inferno, we go out to go in (down to go up), from light into density and density back into the light, birthing ourselves as humans and then back inward again. At some point in our human mid-life, when we've finished honing our containers, we begin a much deeper inner realm journey by opening to the descending energies of heaven, through all the levels of consciousness, ascending back to Unity.

Reflections: How do these concepts or states of being reflect Unity?

Self-Affinity	Individuation
Integration	Heaven or Sky
Sovereignty	Center
Balance	Gaia or Earth

Self-Inquiry: How are you creating community: are you self-serving or in a state of self-denial? Are you anchored in self-affinity? Do you seek balance and individuation? What part of you is known, both to yourself and the outside world; what part is unknown?

The Organic Body

Birth

Your body is a master alchemist, offering you numinous gifts of feeling. The wind breezing through your hair; rain dropping gently on your face; solar flames of passion in your heart; warm sand yielding under your feet; and an etheric mantle covering your skin. Enjoy these physical sensations, and remember, deep inside there are many kindred and even subtler forms awakening greater experiences.

Sacred Body Wisdom

Like the bark, roots, the branches, leaves and core of the **Aspen Tree,** you are a vital, intricate, and co-creative system of physiology with the power to engage the elements and alchemical healing from within.

The *Organic Body* is your physical body, all its physiological systems and their elemental relationships, both internally and externally. In this context it can be seen as simply physiological, or in a deeper sense, as it is connected to the wind, rain, soil and sun. Your body is a sacred vessel; a chalice for your soul and spiritual energies.

DaVinci's **Vitruvian Man** symbolizes the natural world, its five elements, and human connections to three sacred geometrical shapes: the pentagram, the circle and the square.

Your organic body has many systems—endocrine, neurological, musculoskeletal, cardio-respiratory, and lymph-digestive systems correspond to the five primary *Sacred Cisterns* and subtle bodies which are all part of your blueprint.

Your Body

Respiratory System	Circulatory System
Digestive System	Musculoskeletal System
Nervous System	Endocrine System

Your Blueprint
The cells in your physical body were created by the etheric body or blueprint, which is inextricably woven into and through your physiology. Imagine wearing a body suit that is woven through your skin, into your vital organs and bones.

Sacred Body Wisdom

Nature
Air, Fire, Water, Earth, Ether

Energetic Connections
The *Organic Body* is directly connected to *Unity* and three other *Sacred Gateways*. For additional information, read about the following sacred symbols:

Triquetra—Unity
Pentacle—The Elements
Rose—Sacred Cisterns
Sacred Spiral—Rivers & Streams

The Mystic's Journey
The *Sacred Gateway* of the *Organic Body* opens with the merger of your parents seeds, takes you through the womb time, your first breath and into early life. It synchronizes with your energy field; awakening and filling the body, moving through its every cell and anchors fully as you embrace the divine within.

Respiration-Air   Circulation-Water
Digestion-Fire   Restoration-Earth
Communication-Ether

Your Map
The *Organic Body* theme unfolds in the 1st wisdom ring at the beginning of life on earth. Once through the *Sacred Gateway*, there are 5 *stepping stones* of evolution in this theme.

Reflections

How do these concepts or states of being reflect your relationship with your body?

-The blueprint creates the physical body
-Respiration-Air: Air Alchemizes Inspiration
-Digestion-Fire: Fire Alchemizes Transformation
-Circulation-Water: Water Alchemizes Emotion & Creates Awareness where there was only Unconsciousness
-Restoration-Earth: Earth Alchemizes Healing

Self-Inquiry

Are you looking at your health and wellbeing in a solely physical manner or do you find ways to expand your health and well being into and beyond what you can see or touch? Do you see yourself as simply a body or a soul that happens to live in the body and is connected to all other parts of the natural world?

Respiration

Air

The Eastern winds of spirit blow through your body, provoking you to meet its rhythms. Inside, your felt sense heightens, your heart beats in tune with the elements, and your awareness is piqued as the current of your own breath, dances with inspiration.

Sacred Body Wisdom

Sacred Symbolism: *Alchemical Symbol-Air Element*

Your Body: Breath, Heart, Lungs

Your Blueprint: Inspiration, **Eastern Wind**

Nature: The Wind

Practice: Lay on your back, close your eyes and breathe. Notice where you are most receptive as the breath moves in and out.

Self-Reflection: How do you feel when you breathe consciously?

Digestion

Fire

Fire is the alchemical wand of spirit. Held high and burning brightly, it shows the way. It bushwhacks the trail and burns away its dross, clearing the path. Fire is the light—the life-giving property of the sun, both within and without. Fire is powerfully transformative—crucial in digesting food; metabolizing emotions, thoughts, the overloads of every day life, old habits and programming.

Sacred Body Wisdom

Sacred Symbolism: *Alchemical Symbol-Fire Element*

Your Body: Detox & Digestive Organs, Metabolism

Your Blueprint: Transformation, **Southern Sun**

Nature: The Sun

Practice: Expand your belly as you inhale, relax it as you exhale, sensing the warmth of the Sun inside.

Self-Reflection: Can you create enough space in your abdomen to digest all your thoughts and ideas?

Circulation

Water

These are the inner rivers of efference—carrying oxygen through the blood to all parts of the body; and afference—carrying waste material through the lymphatic system for cleansing and back to the blood for nourishment. Water transmutes emotions, carrying them from the unconscious and subconscious realms into consciousness and release.

Sacred Body Wisdom

Sacred Symbolism: *Alchemical Symbol-Water Element*

Your Body: Kidneys, Blood, Veins, Arteries & Lymphatic Vessels

Your Blueprint: Transmutes Emotions to Consciousness, **Western Sea**

Nature: The Rain

Practice: Jiggle and shake your body, sensing the circulation of the fluids inside.

Self-Reflection: How does this exercise change the way you feel about yourself? Where do you feel most open?

Restoration

Earth

Reborn of our ancestors' earthen ashes, our strength and vitality spring from the deep red well of bone marrow and its eternal stream of blood cells.

Sacred Body Wisdom

Sacred Symbolism: *Alchemical Symbol-Earth Element*

Your Body: Bones, Marrow, Muscle, Tendons, Ligaments

Your Blueprint: Healing, **Northern Cave**

Nature: The Earth

Practice: Gently play your body drum to call forth your deepest healing alchemy.

Self Reflection: Where else can you feel the shift of energy in your body?

Communication

Ether

When you open your body to the rhythms of spirit, you encourage the bright and subtle conference that can only occur when you call-in the divine, descending energies that connect your mind and heart through your inner voice.

Sacred Body Wisdom

Sacred Symbolism: *Alchemical Symbol-Ether Element*

Your Body: Nerves & Endocrine Glands

Your Blueprint: Body-Spirit Communication, **As Above, So Below**

Nature: Spiritual Essence

Practice: Sense the space around you, your body, the space around your body; the room and space of the room. Find yourself inside these spaces.

Self Reflection: Are you in center: the center of your own space, the center of your head, your centerline, the center of your aura?

The Elements

Cardinal Alchemy

Your personal essence is an expression of the Earth's seasonal rhythms and cycles, an allegory of nature's imprint in the DNA of all things. Its elemental texture weaves through your health and healing journey, connecting the dots between breath and inspiration; blood and the tides; digestion and wisdom; the still-strength in your bones, and the generation of eternal life force.

Sacred Body Wisdom

The **Elements** and their related directionals are the primary alchemical forces of nature you know as air, fire, water and earth, as well as ether. This blueprint—home to your subtle anatomy, and creator of the energetic frequency for your organs, endocrine and nervous systems, is delicately intertwined with each earthly element and woven through you.

Human healing is inextricably linked to the Earth's healing—your auric field influenced and linked to the threads of planet Earth's blueprint. Each step on the planet's surface is a step upon the human blueprint; each breath you take flows across the winds and through the rivers upon her surface; the rhythm of your heart is an echo of the beat from the womb of the Mother.

The Pentacle is a symbol of your deepest knowledge for transmutation and healing. It reminds you that your human form is connected to nature, the elements and the other worlds. Nature's elements and directions are honored and celebrated at all stages of the harvest and planting seasons with each turn of the Wheel of the Year. Notice the pentacle inside the center of the morning glory.

Your Body
Each physiological system is a hologram of your subtle anatomy in the blueprint. The elements are subtler, and yet more readily available in the blueprint.

Your Blueprint
The Elements theme represents the subtle body, or blueprint.

Sacred Body Wisdom

Nature
Primary Seasons, Growth Cycles, Planting & Harvest Seasons, Directions, Elements

Energetic Connections
The Elements theme is directly connected to *Unity*, the *Organic Body*, *Sacred Cisterns* and *Windows to the Soul*. Read about the following *Sacred Gateways* for general connections to the *Elements* theme:

Triquetra—Unity
Vitruvian Man—Organic Body
Roses—Sacred Cisterns
Wheel of Life—Window to the Soul

The Mystic's Journey
The *Sacred Gateway* of *The Elements* theme opens first to inspiration in the east. It then moves into transformation at the southern point, emotional cleansing and balancing in the west, and restoration in the north, going into the womb of the Earth Mother at winter, taking time for inner reflection and remembrance of the earthly and heavenly energies flowing through all things. Last, it moves into the integrated state of everything above is reflected below.

Eastern Wind	Southern Sun
Western Sea	Northern Cave
As Above, So Below	

Sacred Body Wisdom

Your Map
On the way back to center or *Unity*, the Elements theme unfolds in the 2nd wisdom ring, at the second level on the evolutionary path. Here, through the 5 elemental *stepping stones*, we begin learn about our connections to nature and the elements; that we are more than a body, and have no real power over nature, yet are primordially connected and have incredible power with it.

Reflections
How do these concepts and states of being reflect your relationship with your body?

Air is Wind is East is Spring
Fire is Sun is South is Summer
Water is Rain is the Sea is West is Autumn
Earth is Soil is North is Winter
Ether is Spirit is Above & Below

Self-Inquiry
Can you feel the elements in your body? How do you feel when you stand barefoot in the mud, in the rain, under the heat of the noonday sun, or when a gentle breeze blows across your skin? How does the water circulate within you; how does the fire metabolize your fuel; how do your feet anchor you; how does your breath inspire you? Where does each element create most sensation in your body, or trigger your felt sense?

Eastern

Wind

A time of resurrection and rebirth—the candles of spirit light the way out of the long nights of Winter. The groundhog rises to its purpose. Bright green shoots from underground bulbs breakthrough, and enthusiasm rides in on the first breezes of Spring.

Sacred Body Wisdom

Sacred Symbolism: *Yellow-Green Morning Glory*

Your Body: Breath, Respiration

Your Blueprint: Mental Body, New Beginnings

Nature: Wind, Spring, Air

Practice: Stand in the east where the wind clears away the dross, making space to begin anew. Now relax, breathing softly in the back of your throat. Listen to sounds of the wind inside your throat tunnel.

Self Reflection: How can you use your breath to alchemize your thoughts, beliefs and ideas; your internal environment?

Southern

Sun

The Sun's Summer flame burns away the chill of winter, offering opportunities for cellular transmutation and spiritual alchemy. Summer fires burn deep inside you—metabolism, digestion, the fire of spirit and daily alchemy as you create and destroy the energy of your past experiences.

Sacred Body Wisdom

Sacred Symbolism: *Orange-Red Morning Glory*

Your Body: Digestion & Metabolism

Your Blueprint: Astral Body, Transformation

Nature: Sun, Summer, Fire

Practice: Facing south, dance in the streams of the Sun's golden rays as they touch your skin and nourish your enthusiasm.

Self Reflection: How can you use your inner fire to alchemize internal energies and more fully embrace the spirit inside?

Western

Sea

Gently ebbing tides carry you out to the farther shores in Autumn, where you are cleansed before those currents flood, returning you homeward again. The water element serves as transportation routes for the health and emotional well-being of the planet, moving out stagnancy much like the lymph vessels in your body.

Sacred Body Wisdom

Sacred Symbolism: *Indigo-Teal Morning Glory*

Your Body: Lymph, blood, circulation

Your Blueprint: Etheric Body, Psycho-Spiritual, Devotion

Nature: Oceans, Fall, Waterways

Practice: Facing west, imagine you are standing at the edge of the sea, sensing the gentle pull of the waves, the ground disappearing from under your feet. Allow your breath to follow the rhythms of the tides, pooling in your heart.

Self Reflection: How can you use your awareness of the sea inside to alchemize your emotions?

Northern

Cave

Resting inside the womb of the mother, deep inside her earthen cave, you restore yourself as Winter beckons you further inward. Rest, rejuvenate and grow in the quiet safety of nature's womb.

Sacred Body Wisdom

Sacred Symbolism: *Green-Red Morning Glory*

Your Body: Bones, Marrow, Muscles, Tendons & Ligaments

Your Blueprint: Physical Body, Healing & Integration

Nature: The Land, Winter, Earth

Practice: Face north and sense your body under the cloak of darkness—deep in the cavern of the energy field around you—quietly waiting to emerge into the light.

Self Reflection: How can you use your inner earth element to break free of old habits and outdated patterns? How does the idea of the northern cave in winter help you to integrate new patterns?

As Above So Below

Heaven & Gaia

Two triangles merge to create a six-pointed star, calling heaven to earth, making space in its center for the human heart to reside. Spirit is reflected in body and body in spirit. Your body is a sacred hologram of spiritual energy. Open your body to spirit.

Sacred Body Wisdom

Sacred Symbolism: *Indigo-Teal Morning Glory*

Your Body: The Body is a Spiritual Hologram

Your Blueprint: Spiritual Body, Meeting of Earth & Sky

Nature: Pure Alchemy

Practice: Breathe in a beam of golden light connecting heaven to earth through your body. Feel it moving between your head and tail.

Self Reflection: How do you reflect heaven and earth inside you? How can you find more divinity in your life on Earth?

Sacred Cisterns

Subtle Bodies

Your human journey begins in two places, split between earth and heaven, body and soul. Traveling the seas of life, you first watch your body from the heavens, and as you grow into that body, you begin to see heaven from earth. Standing here, you can open fully to spirit, once more feeling heaven's descent, like a waterfall of light upon you. As it pools at your feet, you begin the ascent through the veils once again.

Sacred Body Wisdom

Sacred Cisterns correspond to five subtle bodies and the central channel that benchmarks the middle way. On this journey, you embrace your divinity by ascending through the veils of consciousness or by allowing higher vibrations to descend into your human beingness. These 5 centers can also be linked to the elements, human physiology, the chakra system, the pranic tube, and the mystical journey itself as it branches out, meandering to both sides of center on its way to divinity.

The Rose is a sacred symbol of beauty, and like the petals on a lotus flower, its multiple layers of color and vibration indicate the various levels of consciousness and wisdom you explore on your inner journey.

Your Blueprint
The Sacred Cisterns represent key parts of your subtle anatomy. Each cistern in this theme relates to an energy center (inside of which exist 1-2 chakras). All are related to different elements, subtle and physical body systems.

Your Body
-All *Sacred Cisterns* relate to specific physiological systems
-Physical Body-Musculoskeletal System- Earth
-Etheric Body-Circulatory System-Water
-Astral Body-Digestive System-Fire
-Mental Body -Respiratory System-Air
-Spiritual Body-Nervous System-Ether

Nature
The Elements   The Planets

Sacred Body Wisdom

Energetic Connections
Sacred Cisterns are directly connected to *Unity, The Organic Body, The Elements, Rivers & Streams, Soul to Soul* and *The Mystical Journey* themes. Read about the following *Sacred Gateways* for general connections to the *Sacred Cisterns* theme:

Triquetra—Unity
Vitruvian Man—Organic Body
Pentacle—The Elements
Sacred Spiral—Rivers & Streams
Flower of Life—Soul to Soul
Qabala—Mystical Journey

The Mystic's Journey
This *Sacred Gateway* opens onto the middle road, which guides you vertically through the central channel or pillar. Moving from the Lower, into the Middle and then to the Upper Realms, you develop relationships with various stages of your evolution:

Physical Body
Etheric Body
Astral Body
Mental Body
Spiritual Body

Your Map
There are 8 *stepping stones* in the *Sacred Cisterns* theme within the 3rd ring of wisdom.

Reflections
How do these concepts and states of being reflect your relationship with your body?

Each *Sacred Cistern* is also anchored horizontally from the spinal area in the physical body, as well as the subtle, spiritual realms of your energy field. Each energy center becomes larger as it emanates outward.

-*Physical Body*—Feet & 1st Chakras; Earth Portal
-*Etheric Body*—2nd & 3rd Chakras; Creative Portal
-*Astral Body*—3rd & 4th Chakras; Vitality Portal
-*Mental Body*—5th & 6th Chakras; Wisdom Portal
-*Spiritual Body*—7th & 8th Chakras; Cosmic Portal
-*Lower World*—Mystical & Underworld
-*Middle World*—Human & Material World
-*Upper World*—Intellectual & Spiritual World

Self-Inquiry
Where are you on your path? Do you allow yourself to meander, to leap and even to fall? Are you opening your body to spirit, allowing divinity to descend, or are you striving, maybe struggling, to climb the ascension ladder?

Physical Body

Felt Senses

When you feel, see or know the earth point under and surrounding your feet, you open the gateway between the material world and the magical kingdoms of the lower world—Faery, Avalon, the Elementals.

Sacred Body Wisdom

Sacred Symbolism: *Red Rose*

Your Body: Feet & Legs

Your Blueprint: Feet & 1st Chakras, **Earth Energy**

Nature: Felt Senses, Lower World

Practice: Call the Earth's energy into the bottom of your feet as you root yourself into its center.

Self Reflection: What are the differences between the moments when you are grounded and those in which you are not?

Etheric Body

Spiritual Blueprint

The energetic pattern for your body's cellular structure lies here in the etheric body, and is inextricably woven into the fabric of your physiology, your health and well-being. Home to human emotions, this energy portal is also a conduit for body-spirit communication. This is your blueprint!

Sacred Body Wisdom

Sacred Symbolism: *Blue Rose*

Your Body: Sexual Organs, Pancreas & Adrenal Glands.

Your Blueprint: 2nd & 3rd Chakras, **Creative Energy**

Nature: Spiritual Blueprint

Practice: Breathe compassion and strength into your belly and out into your etheric body. Use this energy to cleanse your cellular blueprint.

Self Reflection: How do you sense your blueprint and its connection to your cells? Can you sense the difference in your vitality when your blueprint is clear?

Astral Body

Imaginal Teleport

Your chest is filled with heart, breath and incredible power to transport you through the inner dimensions. This dream portal opens deep into the imaginal planes where the mundane and spiritual realms are bridged by self-affinity and total surrender. The core of your immune system, this is home to your soul and the commitment you made to your physical body at birth.

Sacred Body Wisdom

Sacred Symbolism: *Orange-Yellow Rose*

Your Body: Heart, Lungs, Thymus

Your Blueprint: 3rd & 4th Chakras, **Vital Energy**

Nature: Imaginal Teleport

Practice: Create the image of a small golden sun beneath your breastbone, expanding until it fills your whole chest. Allow it to fill your body, expanding out to fill your aura. Repeat this with all colors.

Self Reflection: What most assists you in finding the sweetness of self-affinity?

Mental Body

Thoughts & Beliefs

Soaring through the airy realms of your higher mind into the psycho-spiritual world of co-creation, your inner voice calls down the stars from above, reminding you that you are the Cosmos.

Sacred Body Wisdom

Sacred Symbolism: *Indigo-Purple Rose*

Your Body: Brain, Thyroid, Pituitary & Pineal Glands, Thalamus, Hypothalamus

Your Blueprint: 5th & 6th Chakras

Nature: Thoughts & Beliefs

Practice: Breathe into your nose, deep into the center of your head. Exhale down your spine and into the Earth's center.

Self Reflection: How can you use your breath to spread the inspiration of your higher mind throughout your whole being?

Spiritual Body

Soul Memories

Don your spiritual body suit to surf the etheric waves, riding its crests to your soul point above. From this place you have complete autonomy in any realm. Ride through the tunnel, under the eaves of the cosmic gateway.

Sacred Body Wisdom

Sacred Symbolism: *Silver Rose*

Your Body: Pineal Gland, Neo Cortex-Cerebrum

Your Blueprint: 7th & 8th Chakras, **Cosmic Energy**

Nature: Soul Memory

Practice: Open the cosmic gates, calling down the golden suns of higher vibration. Feel the energy pouring through you, flooding your humanity with divinity.

Self Reflection: When and where are you most available to your spiritual energies?

Lower World

Realm of Rebirth

Going within, you slide down the root system of the ancient tree giants, into the underworld where magic is born, across the mystical sea, in the lands beyond the mists.

Sacred Body Wisdom

Sacred Symbolism: *Redwood Tree Roots*

Your Body: Feet, Legs, Marrow, Mitochondria

Your Blueprint: Shadow & Re-birth, **Primordial Power**

Nature: Root Systems, Natural Springs, the Primordial Soup

Practice: Sit next to your favorite tree. Imagine your body is linked to the root bed, into the magical worlds below.

Self Reflection: Can you smell, feel, touch or hear the life deep underground? Can you imagine it? How does it look?

Middle World

Human & Nature Spirits

From both inner and outer perspectives, this realm grows like the trunk of the redwood, into the earth through its roots, and into the heavens through its branches. Only from here can you effect the changes needed for evolution and ascension.

Sacred Body Wisdom

Sacred Symbolism: *Redwood Tree Trunk*

Your Body: Torso, Spinal Column

Your Blueprint: Humans and Nature Spirits, **Body Currents**

Nature: Wisdom Rings, Nourishment

Practice: Sit comfortably, engage and release your pelvic floor muscles several times. Feel your connection to the center of the Earth.

Self Reflection: Imagine you are a tree. Are you more in tune with the upper or lower realms of your tree? Can you be in the middle world and still experience the energies from above and below?

Upper World

Angelic Realm

Your branches reach high into the cosmos and the upper realms. They are only as certain as your roots are strong and anchored, and your trunk is both flexible and solid.

Sacred Body Wisdom

Sacred Symbolism: *Redwood Tree Branches*

Your Body: Arms & Head, Higher Mind

Your Blueprint: Co-Creation, Star Beings, **Spiritual Essence**

Nature: Tree Branches, the Polestar & Big Dipper

Practice: Absorb the blue of the sky, the light of the stars and the gold of the sun, filling yourself with the jewels of the heavens. Now exhale and release your stagnancy, giving back to the heavens.

Self-Reflection: What helps you to access and envision the energies of the spirit world descending into your body and its energy field? What inhibits this ability?

Rivers & Streams

Esoteric Anatomy

Acquaint your energy intelligence with the rivers and streams inside your body: the many subtle energy channels called nadis, meridians and elemental lines. Like veins, arteries and nerves in your physical body, these subtle channels source, move, contain, and pool the effervescent essences that nourish you on the mystical journey of life. Fortify their constitution with awareness, sensation, and

ultimately expanded consciousness, by following the spiraling, watercourse way.

Rivers and Streams are the subtle body *channels and containers* for your inner currents—both subtle and physical. The effervescent essences flowing through you are sourced, held and channeled by the inner rivers and stream beds. As channels, they nourish, support and guide you on the mystical journey of life. Peak your awareness; become acquainted with the rivers and streams inside.

The **Sacred Spiral** tells us that all energy and watercourses are both circular and multidimensional. Circulatory routes for fluids and electricity, in nature they are waterways, air, mist and rain, rays of sun, root systems. Energetically they are meridians, vortexes and nadis, moving and carrying life force, into and through your body and energy field.

Your Body
These subtle channels and energy centers are frequency matches to certain parts of the physical body. Among them are nerves, veins and arteries, the endocrine system, alveoli, the spinal column and lymphatic vessels—holograms of your etheric body blueprint.

Your Blueprint
Much like the chakras or cisterns, *Rivers & Streams* are channels and energy centers that exist in the subtle body(s). They expand from there, outward into the rest of your auric field.

Sacred Body Wisdom

Nature
The *Rivers & Streams* are containers for the elemental nature of our internal energies and spiritual forces like chi or kundalini. They are bays, channels, eddies, estuaries, as well as rivers and streams. Explore the specific references to these bodies of water in the symbolism of each card.

Energetic Connections
Rivers & Streams are directly linked to *Unity, The Organic Body, The Mystical Journey, Windows to the Soul,* and *Gateways to the Heights* themes. For more information, read about these *Sacred Gateways* symbols and themes:

Triquetra—Unity
Vitruvian Man—Organic Body
Qabala—Mystical Journey
Triple Spiral—Gateways to the Heights
Wheel of Life—Windows to the Soul

The Mystic's Journey
As the *Sacred Gateway* of *Rivers & Streams* opens, you begin to acknowledge energy—a greater level of divinity in your body. You learn, or begin to know, that it is not only in and around you—it is you. At this stage you begin to ask how you can further experience your spirituality.

Vital Vessels	Sources
Anchorage	The Riverbed
Tributaries	Streams
Wellsprings	Pools of Energy

Sacred Body Wisdom

Your Map

The *Rivers & Streams* theme has 8 stepping stones in the 4th ring of wisdom.

Reflections

How do these energies reflect the relationship you have with your body?

Connections to Earth & Heaven	Nadis
The Nervous System	Chakras
Life Force	Nerve & Blood Plexi
Endocrine Glands	Creative Expression
Nourishment	Your Aura
Meridians	Polarity Grid
Luminosity	

Self-Inquiry

Can you feel your blood flowing through your body? How does your breath feel as it moves through your body into the cells? How do you feel when your nervous system is balanced or imbalanced? Can you viscerally sense or feel the difference between yourself and another person; can you feel the similarities? Can you feel the difference between being grounded and ungrounded? How does being in communication with the divine manifest in your physical body?

Vital Vessels

Circulatory Systems

Your organic body is born with a certain level of vitality that courses through the highway of veins, electrical circuitry, other circulatory vessels and transport routes for nourishment.

Sacred Body Wisdom

Sacred Symbolism: *Atlantic Bridge, Scotland*

Your Body: Nerves, Veins & Arteries

Your Blueprint: Vitality, Chakra Plexi, **Body Currents**

Nature: Canals

Practice: Stand with your feet comfortably apart, bend your knees, gently bouncing your body while you hum!

Self Reflection: Can you feel your blood and lymph pulsing through their vessels?

Sources

Earth & Cosmic Energy Channels

Earth and cosmic energies flow deep in the marrow of your bones through channels like Earth's aquifers and underground waterways. When you breathe in from above and below, you can feel the flood of the divine, even in the densest of places.

Sacred Body Wisdom

Sacred Symbolism: *Parallel Paths in Glencoe Scotland*

Your Body: Cerebrum & Pelvic Floor, Feet

Your Blueprint: Earth & Cosmic Energy, Feet, Root & Crown Chakras

Nature: Mountain Streams & Paths

Practice: Feel the earth energy flowing upward into the lower body, cosmic energy flowing downward through your spinal column to meet it in your abdominal cauldron.

Self Reflection: How well do you navigate the inner terrain of these energy streams? Do you match their commitment to get where you are going?

Anchorage

Chakra Plexi

You will take full ownership of your body by anchoring your energy in the primary cauldrons at the chest, belly and head. This becomes particularly sensate when you surrender to the flow of energy moving in and out.

Sacred Body Wisdom

Sacred Symbolism: *Rock Inlet, Cornwall, England*

Your Body: Joints, Nerve Roots & Plexi

Your Blueprint: Vortexes, Chakras & Energy Portals

Nature: Sea Caves and Caverns

Practice: Draw golden lines of connection from the floor of any room, building or other space, into earth's center.

Self Reflection: How does grounding a space help you to remain anchored in your body?

The Riverbed

Sun, Moon, Centerline

A golden river of light flows upward through the center of your body between head and tail, awakening and encouraging healing. Sun and moon energies split and meander downward, manifesting in subtle and physical realms along the way.

Sacred Body Wisdom

Sacred Symbolism: *The Glastonbury Tor*

Your Body: Autonomic Nervous System, Spinal Column

Your Blueprint: Primordial Power, Central Channel, Pranic Tube, Primary Nadis

Nature: Sacred Rivers & Parallel Streams

Practice: Feel the rivers and streams flowing down the back of your spine from your head to your pelvis, and back up to your head again. Now reverse the direction, feeling the energy moving up your spine and then back downward.

Self Reflection: Can you sense the tides and currents of the riverbed in your body?

Tributaries

Lesser Nadis

Imagine thousands of tiny rivulets moving energy through your body—life forces, the whispers of your soul. See their corporeal reflections in the delicate capillaries and wispy nerve periphery, fluidly inspiring the messages of your body's wisdom. Primal life forces run through these secondary connections off the main river, nourishing your consciousness and eliminating unconscious, stagnant energies.

Sacred Body Wisdom

Sacred Symbolism: *Red & White Springs, England*

Your Body: Peripheral Nervous System, Veins & Capillaries

Your Blueprint: Life Forces, Prana Apana

Nature: Tributaries & Underground Springs

Practice: Inhale up from your feet, into your head. Exhale down again, sending a gentle wave of energy through every cell of your body.

Self Reflection: How does your breath feel as you move and contain it inside you?

Streams

Meridians & Fields of Energy

A stream has no content without its shape. All riverbeds have a grid or system of smaller channels that feed and link to the nearby waterways in creeks and streams. Similar links between your central channel—the primary river of energy that parallels your spinal column, and the lesser energy streams deep inside you, create unique connections within your physical and subtle bodies, and energy field.

Sacred Body Wisdom

Sacred Symbolism: *Blarney Rock Waterfall, Ireland*

Your Body: Fascia, Electromagnetic Field

Your Blueprint: Divine Matrix, Aura, Meridians, Polarity Grid

Nature: Water falling & moving over rocks.

Practice: Breathe into your central channel; exhale, creating little streams through your body with your breath, awakening feeling everywhere inside you. Inhale the streams back to the main river again.

Self Reflection: Can you sense your internal rocks as the breath moves effortlessly over, through and around them?

Wellsprings
Creative Channels

Creative energy springs from three places: the Crown, Throat and Sacral Chakras. Their qualities are procreative, manifest, and co-creative energies that move through every cell of your body and every inch of your subtle anatomy.

Sacred Body Wisdom

Sacred Symbolism: *Chalice Well, Glastonbury, England*

Your Body: Birth, Sexual Energies

Your Blueprint: Creative Energy, Chakras & Arm Channels

Nature: Wells, Springs & Natural Fountains

Practice: Feel the spring in your lower cauldron. Its waters fountain up through your body pooling in your throat and at the crown of your head. Feel the energy spilling down through the pools again like a waterfall.

Self Reflection: Can you sense the energy of these three chakras: 2nd, 5th, 7th? Can you envision the flow of energy between them?

Pools of Energy
Cauldron of Creation

The light of the golden flame in your mind's eye shows you the way to the shimmering pool of energy that holds your spiritual essence. Once there, you sense the knowledge of the universe flowing through your body, speaking the language of your soul. Your crown heals everything beneath.

Sacred Body Wisdom

Sacred Symbolism: *Pacific Ocean Eddy, Northern California*

Your Body: Crown of the Head, Brain, Meninges

Your Blueprint: Crown Chakra, **Spiritual Essence**

Nature: Eddies and Pools

Practice: Massage the top of your head with your fingertips to awaken your crown.

Self Reflection: Can you transmute or change the heaviness in your head by bringing awareness to a place beyond thought, into the void of creation?

Soul to Soul

The Language of Spirit

Learn to speak the subtle language of spirit. Your inherent capacity for soul level communication resides at the seat of your wisdom in various intentions, daily choices and creative expressions. It is intuitive! The Flower of Life, symbolized in sacred Celtic knots and in the rose at the labyrinthine center, calls back your knowingness of the limitless and subtle connections you have to all things.

Sacred Body Wisdom

Soul to Soul expresses the many subtle ways you connect with your own soul, connect with the divine and your body—its emotions and thoughts; your ability see, feel, and speak with others as spirit, as well as your temporal relationship with the outer world. These subtle communication capabilities exist in the place where your subtle energy and physiological systems meet. Primarily found mirrored within various brain functions, the energy of these qualities moves through your hands and feet, enhancing consciousness, affecting your intentions, and proactivity. Like the power of the waves and currents in the ocean, these qualities are omnipresent.

The **Flower of Life** begins with a single seed of life and grows into a matrix of many seeds. It symbolizes your foundations in and integration with the mineral, plant, animal, human, angelic-spiritual and unknown realms. You begin the conversation between body and spirit with your ability to communicate through subtle channels on physical, mental-emotional and spiritual levels.

Your Body
This theme links primarily to your triune brain: the emotional—mammalian midbrain; the physical brainstem/cerebellum—lower reptilian brain, and the mental—cerebrum or upper brain.

Your Blueprint
Most of your inherent psychic traits are linked to the 5th, 6th & 7th chakras, your energy field and subtle body(s) energies. The brain is a cosmic hologram of the stars in the sky and these subtle facets of your being.

Sacred Body Wisdom

Nature
In this theme we use animal symbolism to reflect the purest vibration of these qualities.

Energetic Connections
Soul to Soul is directly linked to all other *Sacred Body Cards*. For more information, read about the following *Sacred Gateways* and symbols:

Triquetra—Unity
Vitruvian Man—Organic Body
Pentacle—The Elements
Rose—Sacred Cisterns
Sacred Spiral—Rivers & Streams
Qabala—Mystical Journey
Wheel of Life—Windows to the Soul
Triple Spiral—Gateways to the Height

The Mystic's Journey
Now the *Sacred Gateway* opens to your subtle, psychic communications and greater awareness. As you grow into the language of the soul, you open your body further to your spiritual inheritance.

-Connection: Sheep: Confidence
-Origins: Caterpillar: The Fetus, Infancy
-Clear Sight: Peacock: Inner Sight
-Expressions: Jelly Fish: Currents
-Envisioning; Owl: Piercing the Veil
-Consciousness: Swan: Self-Transformation

-Impressions: Pelican: Navigates Emotions, Deep Dives
-Balance: Deer: Grace, Gentle Alertness
-Knowingness: Salmon: Wisdom
-Telepathy: Raven: Wisdom Messenger
-The Witness: Sea Gull: Freedom
-Record Keeper: Whale: Inner Awakening
-Healing: Wolf: Teacher

Your Map
Here, in the *Soul to Soul* theme, you learn the awareness and communication tools of spirit. Its 13 *stepping stones* sit in the 5th wisdom ring—midway between birth and unity.

Reflections
How do these energies and states of being reflect your relationship with yourself and others?

Neutrality	Manifesting Change
Focus	Homeostasis
Clairvoyance	Receptivity
Knowingness	Akashic Records
God's Eye	Free Will
Clairsentience	Spiritual Intentions
Pre-Cognition	Inner Voice
Empathy	Consciousness
Clairaudience	Morphogenetic Fields
Becoming the Witness	Creating & Destroying

Self-Inquiry

Do you embrace, honor and cultivate your intuition, gut feelings, perceptions and interpretations? Do you spend time purposefully creating and envisioning your dreams? Do you intentionally create your own reality? How do you manifest your soul purpose and what do you want out of life?

Connection

Grounding

Walking barefoot increases sensation in your feet. It opens the feet chakras and connects your body to the ground beneath you. When you are aware, you can feel the earth's energy tickling the bottom of your feet, encouraging the energy centers on their soles to open and fill you with life, vitality and presence.

Sacred Body Wisdom

Sacred Symbolism: *Tibetan Deer, Highlands Wildlife Park, Scotland*

Your Body: Feet, Legs, Pelvic Floor, Anchoring

Your Blueprint: Feet Chakras, Root Chakra, **Earth Energy**

Nature: Earth, Sheep

Practice: Lie on your back with your knees bent. Inhale and exhale, gently rocking your tailbone up and down to the rhythm of your breath. Engage and release the pelvic floor muscles as you repeat this movement.

Self-Reflection: Can you enhance your relationship to present time by grounding? How is sure footedness related to your root chakra?

Origins
Chrysalis

Liquid golden light moves gracefully between head and tail as your spinal column vibrates from your pelvis upward, resetting your foundation for health and well-being. Awareness of your physical core is sensation; awareness of your subtle core is your ability to see and know without the senses.

Sacred Body Wisdom

Sacred Symbolism: *North Coast Caterpillar, California*

Your Body: Brainstem, Homeostasis

Your Blueprint: Genetics, Brow Chakra, **Primordial Power, The Riverbed**

Nature: Caterpillar

Practice: Sit upright and gently reach your heart forward, arching your back, and then softening your heart as you round backward, creating a wave-like movement. Move with your breath, slowly and thoughtfully. Close your eyes, feel your body, and know freedom.

Self-Reflection: How does subtle, gentle movement create freedom for you?

Clear Sight

Clarity

Nestled deep in the center of your head are the four pillars of your inner kingdom: pineal, pituitary, thalamus and hypothalamus. When your attention is focused inward and the external senses are withdrawn, you are capable of seeing more clearly—to know the energy of the universe inside.

Sacred Body Wisdom

Sacred Symbolism: *Irish Peacock*

Your Body: Pineal Gland

Your Blueprint: Clairvoyance, Brow & Crown Chakras, **Mental Body**

Nature: Peacock, Tides & Currents

Practice: Lie on your back with eyes closed, your knees bent, arms extended up, and fingertips reaching to the ceiling. Relax your shoulder blades onto the floor. Alternately move one arm overhead and the other to the floor alongside your body. Move slowly in a range of motion that feels comfortable for your body. Move with the rhythm of our breath. Repeat this several times.

Self-Reflection: What do you notice as you perform this exercise? How do these simple, gentle, coordination movements enhance your clarity?

Expressions

Blueprint

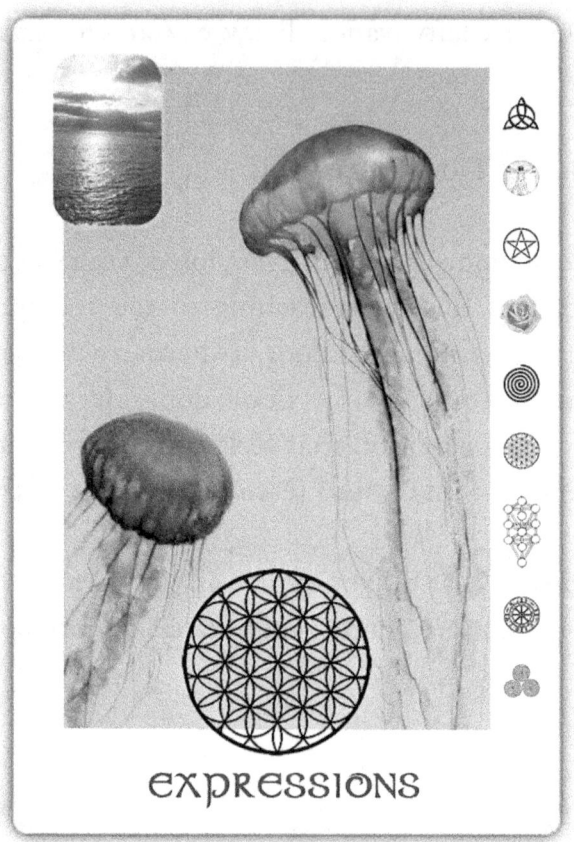

As you relax your body and quiet your mind, you open the wonder-filled space of connection between body and spirit and its authentic expression. Your inner voice matches the frequency of your heart and true essence. As it speaks, you listen. As you listen, your essence expresses.

Sacred Body Wisdom

Sacred Symbolism: *Jelly Fish, Atlanta Aquarium*

Your Body: Hypothalamus, Bio-Regulation

Your Blueprint: Crown Point, Crown Chakra, **Spiritual Body & Spiritual Essence**

Nature: Jelly Fish, Big Dipper

Practice: Lie on your back with your knees bent, gently rolling your knees side to side in rhythm with your breath. Roll your head side to side in the same way. Now combine both movements, repeating several times each direction.

Self-Reflection: How does relaxation and gentle movement play a role in your ability to converse with spirit?

Envisioning

Focus

Your ability to envision is limitless. Your ability to create change is also limitless. When you create and hold a picture of life that suits your soul, you align with your purpose and create the life that is really yours. You create each day with intention at its center.

Sacred Body Wisdom

Sacred Symbolism: *Highlands Owl, Scotland*

Your Body: Visual Cortex, Optic Chiasma, Pineal & Pituitary Glands

Your Blueprint: Brow & Crown Chakras, **Visualization**

Nature: Owl, Polestar, Ursa Major

Practice: Close your eyes, envisioning a sacred nature symbol—the sea, a bee, a flower or a tree, for example. Know that symbol as you hold it in your mind's eye as long as you can.

Self-Reflection: Do you rise each morning with a vision for your day? Do you set an intention as you drift off to sleep at night, knowing that your dreams will help you create your next steps?

Consciousness

Spiritual Intentions

Your consciousness expands with awareness and experience, unlocking the realm of awareness in your unconscious mind. You cannot see beyond the choice you haven't yet made. Learn, interact and expand, as each new experience opens even more awareness, creating a new level of consciousness, and ultimately an opportunity for another choice.

Sacred Body Wisdom

Sacred Symbolism: *Swan, Oban, Scotland*

Your Body: Thalamus, Frontal Lobe, Self-Awareness, Reasoning & Discernment

Your Blueprint: Brow & Crown Chakras, **Spiritual Body, Self-Inquiry & Reflection**

Nature: Swan, Water

Practice: Sit quietly breathing, noticing how your breath moves your pelvic floor. Continue breathing, noticing how your breath moves your diaphragm and your head bones. Sit for a few minutes with your attention on these places.

Self-Reflection: Can you embrace the simplicity and effortlessness of this practice?

Impressions

Empathy

When you observe life with your attention inside the center of your head, your inner eye opens. From here, you will find a place of neutrality in your emotional and mental impressions. Your perceptions are unaffected by the chemistry of past experience and stressful memories. You learn to create and embrace your experiences from a higher state of being.

Sacred Body Wisdom

Sacred Symbolism: *Pelican, Baja, Mexico*

Your Body: Emotional Responses, Amygdala

Your Blueprint: Brow, Heart and Sacral Chakras, **Creative Energy,** Clairsentience

Nature: Pelican, Large Bodies of Water

Practice: Sit at the edge of an armless chair. Breathe in, lengthen your spine and twist at the waist moving your upper body around to the left, allowing your opposite sitting bone to lift. Very gently pull yourself further with your right hand on your left knee. Exhale back to center. Repeat slowly and thoughtfully on each side several times.

Self-Reflection: How do you manage your energy, your boundaries, and your relationships? Do you balance and conserve, give it all away, or do you put up walls and hoard it?

Balance

Neutrality

Your inner equilibrium is formed by interpretations of your perceptions and your ability to discern and utilize the energy of those experiences in the moment. When you detach from the negative energies of the past, neutrality and balance become more available.

Sacred Body Wisdom

Sacred Symbolism: *Deer, Northern California*

Your Body: Brain, Higher Consciousness

Your Blueprint: Throat, Brow & Crown Chakras, **Visualization, Awakening Awareness**

Nature: Deer

Practice: Sit on a throne in the center of your head. Envision a golden rose in your hand and begin to dust and clear your inner kingdom.

Self-Reflection: Can you find neutrality and ease with all things: no qualifications of good or bad; hot or cold; comfort or discontent; intensity or indifference?

Knowingness

Receptivity

If you can empty your mind for only a moment, you will experience the knowledge of the Universe flowing through you.

Sacred Body Wisdom

Sacred Symbolism: *Salmon of Knowledge*

Your Body: Pituitary

Your Blueprint: Mediumship, Brow & Crown Chakras, Awakening Awareness

Nature: Salmon, The Sea

Practice: Breathe in to feel your body. Breathe out to release any tension. Breathe in to become more present; breathe out any past-time energy. Breathe in to fill the center of your head; breathe out to release anything that is not your own.

Self-Reflection: Does an empty mind seem unachievable? Can you allow your thoughts to move aside as you experience that moment between breaths?

Telepathy

Transmission

Listen intently for the call of benevolence. The messenger comes alive when you listen to your inner voice. Speak and respond gently with your soul to receive and transmit higher frequencies in the world outside.

Sacred Body Wisdom

Sacred Symbolism: *Raven, Glastonbury, England*

Your Body: The Brain: Pituitary, Temporal Lobes and Cerebellum.

Your Blueprint: Clairaudience, Messenger, Throat, Brow & Crown Chakras, **Awakening Awareness, Self-Healing & Mastery**

Nature: Raven, Outcropping

Practice: Imagine tossing your negative, circular, repeating thoughts into the air. Watch them burst into a trillion little particles, transforming into a brilliant light show. Or, you could toss them down the garbage disposal and switch it on.

Self-Reflection: Have you ever considered that your thoughts can override your emotions and how you see yourself? How about your attitudes—can your thoughts pull the wool over your own eyes, hiding your behaviors from yourself?

The Witness

God's Eye

The fires of curiosity are always lit within the observer. The flame of limitlessness burns eternally within when you walk through life as a witness.

Sacred Body Wisdom

Sacred Symbolism: *Sea Gull, Northern California*

Your Body: Cerebellum, Motor Control and Hard Wiring, Soaring

Your Blueprint: Brow Chakra, God of the Heart, **Self-Healing & Mastery**, **Awakening Awareness**

Nature: Sea Gull, Thermal Lift

Practice: Walk slowly and intentionally as you hold a sacred symbol in your mind's eye. Know you can call it back if it disappears, envisioning the symbol indefinitely.

Self-Reflection: Do you empower yourself to observe and change what you don't like while embracing what you enjoy?

The Record Keeper

Akashic Records

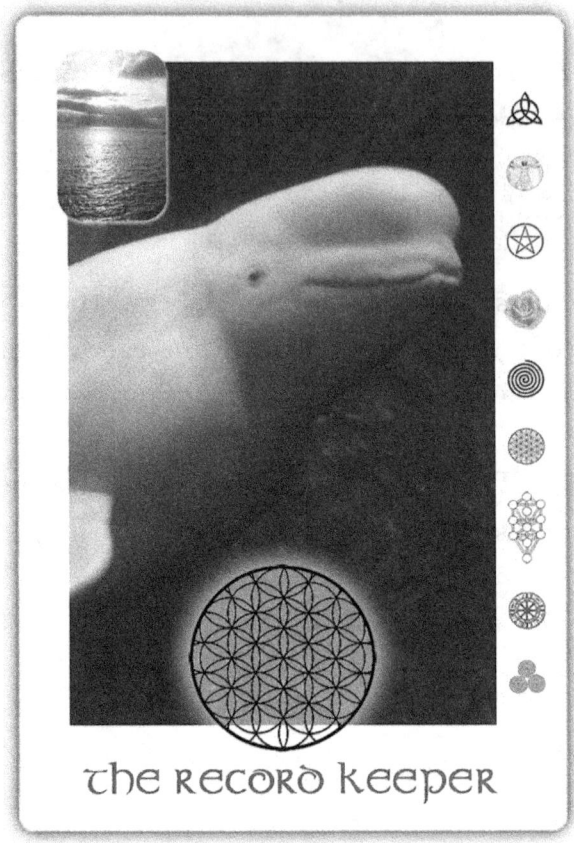

You will find your answers when you are ready and willing to dive deep into the deep into the fathomless sea and unknown spaces, moving beyond time, into the quiet and eternal library at the threshold.

Sacred Body Wisdom

Sacred Symbolism: *Beluga Whale, Atlanta Aquarium*

Your Body: Long Term Memory, Hippocampus & Cerebellum

Your Blueprint: Akashic Records, the Threshold, **Self-Healing & Mastery**

Nature: Whales, Solar Systems Sirius & the Pleiades

Practice: Breathe gently, expanding and contracting your chest, lifting and lowering your breastbone. Each time you exhale, repeat the sound, HAAAA, blowing stagnant air out of your mouth.

Self-Reflection: Do you allow the mental act of knowing to block your inherent wisdom and soul memories?

Healing

Manifesting Change

When you hold your hands out to the world, you let all know you are ready and willing to give, receive and embrace your life.

Sacred Body Wisdom

Sacred Symbolism: *Wolf, Highlands Wildlife Preserve, Scotland*

Your Body: Hands, Receptivity, Non-Resistance

Your Blueprint: Healing, Throat & Hand Chakras, Psychometry, Creating, Manifesting, **Creative Energy, Self-Healing & Mastery**

Nature: Wolves, Family

Practice: Clap your hands, rapidly rub them together creating heat, then bathe yourself in their warmth and transformational healing.

Self-Reflection: Do you take the time—any time at all, to simply touch your body, sincerely connecting to yourself? Do you stop to touch a flower or a tree, run your hands over a beautiful inanimate object? How do these things feel to you?

The Mystical Journey

Pathworking

Unknown until it appears, the journey unfolds with each step and every breath. The search for truth remains a brilliant and eternal, often wild adventure. It meanders along three very different and evolutionary pathways. The middle road of ease and integration appears to be the clearest and most direct route, yet is often unmarked. On either side of center, the solar and lunar paths simultaneously

reflect and repel one another, yet each leads to a different, less traveled route. Each requires degrees of strength and compassion to bridge the crevasse between them.

Men An Tol is a megalithic stone portal. Venture through it and the energy readily transmutes. A search for truth and virtue, a walk toward the silence to find inner knowledge, non-dualism and the depths of primordial wisdom, **The Qabalistic Tree of Life** gives us three options. The center path is quieter, one that is relatively easy and almost perfect, though there are many options, bridges to cross and forks in the road. These paths and their steps are all linked; they are all evolutionary. Without the extremes, learning would be uninspiring and you would never truly know the middle path. In the end, all roads lead back to center.

Your Body
Your body has been created from the same template from which the stars and planets are birthed. Although yours has evolved into a different form, the patterns are, and will continue to be influenced by the galactic pulse and the orbiting planets of at least three solar systems at the time of your birth. As well, each planet in those very same solar systems is formed by and resonates with an elemental vibration and a universal pattern. The Qabalistic Tree of Life is a mystical system or map of potential spiritual paths and related steps through the evolutionary frequencies of ancient symbols and tones, levels of consciousness, angelic, astrological, and Tarot symbolism.

Your Blueprint
The Mystical Journey theme is based on the holograms of the

subtle body. Whatever path you have chosen, you rise through the veils of consciousness, moving from the physical to the etheric and into the spiritual realms. Each stepping-stone along the way corresponds to levels of consciousness and subtle body(s) or energy templates.

Nature
The Mystical Journey is influenced by our solar system, Sun and Moon, and at least two other solar systems within our galaxy—Pleiades and Sirius.

Energetic Connections
The Mystical Journey is linked to all *Sacred Body Cards* and symbols. For more information, read about these *Sacred Gateways* and themes:

Triquetra—Unity
Vitruvian Man—Organic Body
Pentacle—The Elements
Rose—Sacred Cisterns
Sacred Spiral—Rivers & Streams
Flower of Life—Spirit to Spirit
Wheel of Life—Windows to the Soul
Triple Spiral—Gateways to the Heights

The Mystic's Journey
Within the *Sacred Gateway* of *The Mystical Journey*, there are three paths and three choices: one is known; the other two are potential new adventures in evolution. It's up to you to decide where you've already been and where to direct your attention.

Sacred Body Wisdom

Strength-Left   Compassion-Right
Brilliance-Mercury   Evolution-Venus
Vitality-Mars   Expansion-Jupiter
Intelligence-Saturn   Wisdom- Zodiac

Your Map
The Mystical Journey theme takes you to a network of pathways. Upon arrival you choose whether to travel with the guidance of the Moon Mother, the Sun Father, up through center, or some combination of all three routes. *The Mystical Journey* has 9 stepping-stones within the 6th wisdom ring.

Reflections
How do these energies and states of being reflect your relationship with yourself and others?

-Integration or Repelling of Polarities
-The elemental aspects of the planets:
  Mercury—earth & air
  Mars—fire
  Saturn—earth
  Venus—earth
  Jupiter—fire
-The Zodiac-all elements

Self-Inquiry
How do you see yourself maneuvering between strength and compassion, masculine and feminine, negative and positive, fiery and watery interpretations of your life? Do you judge yourself when you are at odds or extremes? Do you struggle to stay on the

middle road, or do you take risks to expand and evolve your knowing and spiritual intelligence?

Strength
Pillar of Justice

The door to inner strength opens when you change your context—entering different or unknown territory. It is a quality you will cultivate when making different choices and taking exploratory risks that nudge you off your normal course.

Sacred Body Wisdom

Sacred Symbolism: *Pillar Ruins, Jerpoint Abbey, Ireland*

Your Body: Action, Resistance, Rebellion, Aggression, Assertion, **Autonomic Nervous System**

Your Blueprint: Mother, Negative Polarity, **Primordial Power, The Riverbed**

Nature: Moon

Practice: Engage and release your lower abdomen and pelvic floor muscles. Try them separately and then simultaneously. Now lift the pelvic floor in an upward motion. Hold it for a breath cycle.

Self Reflection: Become aware of any tendencies to avoid experiencing your essential self, just to stay safe. When do the default modes appear and what are your responses to those habits when they come up?

Compassion

Pillar of Mercy

Compassion is often mistaken as softness, though the steel of the sword forged in fire is more compassionate than sweetness. Many will prefer a gentler path, yet only when it is fueled by strength can it be a real and true expression of relationship and humanity.

Sacred Body Wisdom

Sacred Symbolism: *Glendalough Tower, Wicklow, Ireland*

Your Body: Receptivity, **Autonomic Nervous System**

Your Blueprint: Father, Positive Polarity, **Primordial Power, The Riverbed**

Nature: Sun

Practice: As you breathe deeply into your body, envision the constellations lighting up in your cells.

Self Reflection: Have you cultivated enough self-affinity to be truly compassionate toward the world and other people?

Brilliance

Splendor

Body to spirit communication shines light on your journey inward. Once inside, this newly integrated frequency sends a beacon of light out into the unknown, and opens the door to your next step.

Sacred Body Wisdom

Sacred Symbolism: *Astrological Symbol for Mercury*

Your Body: Communication

Your Blueprint: Mother, **Communication-Ether, Expression**

Nature: Moon

Practice: Breathe into your root chakra, allowing the energy to pool there. Breathe out through the threads of connection into that same chakra in your blueprint. Repeat this with all 7 chakras.

Self Reflection: What is your response to body pain and emotional imbalance? Can you remain neutral without avoiding it completely? Can you be curious without dramatizing it?

Evolution

Victory

If you fall too far into the well of pride, you will miss finding beauty in the mundane, amusement and enthusiasm for the simple things in life. Willingness guides us to the path up the mountain, and supports us along the way. Willfulness may move you through the steeps at faster speeds, yet it is filled with a compulsion to push through and ride over the top of the energies from your past.

Sacred Body Wisdom

Sacred Symbolism: *Astrological Symbol for Venus*

Your Body: Affinity

Your Blueprint: Father, **Connection**

Nature: Sun

Practice: Find ways to request support. Find a mentor or an advisor. Cultivate people in your life who will reflect honestly to you. Journal about your experiences.

Self Reflection: What is the difference between amusement and hilarity; excitement and enthusiasm; surrender and succumbing?

Vitality

Intention

Mars' erect arrow of vitality is in constant search of a target, holding and pinpointing its course with focused precision. Its mission is action: to create. Now is the time to find the seeds of vitality inside your body and utilize that potency to create from the baseline of your spiritual intention. Carefully place your arrow, focus, exhale, draw your bow, and release. Watch as it flies straight to the target's center.

Sacred Body Wisdom

Sacred Symbolism: *Astrological Symbol for Mars*

Your Body: Action

Your Blueprint: Mother, **Primordial Power, Origins**

Nature: Moon

Practice: Experience the clarity of your goals when seen through the lens of spiritual intention. Kindle that fire for some time before you lose yourself in its ideology. Write or draw your visions.

Self Reflection: Do you find yourself becoming lost in ideas and beliefs, goals and affirmations, unable to achieve them? Are your goals and desires based in spiritual intention?

Expansion

Trust

Look closely from a distance. You may be in denial and avoidance, or have a false sense of satisfaction. Be wary of immediate gratification. Expand from a place of rootedness. Find awareness in your crown, and center in your heart.

Sacred Body Wisdom

Sacred Symbolism: *Astrological Symbol for Jupiter*

Your Body: Self-Affinity, Self Trust

Your Blueprint: Father, **Consciousness,** The Witness

Nature: Sun

Practice: Begin and end your day with a simple request to experience and awaken to the ways you are most in denial. Set dream intentions and create a journal for this purpose.

Self Reflection: Do you in any way wear the clothing of someone else's ideas of perfection?

Intelligence

Knowledge

Understanding, direction and focus combine in the cauldron of conscious creation, bringing primal energies into heart, and heart into mind, and the eventual birth of your dreams.

Sacred Body Wisdom

Sacred Symbolism: *Astrological Symbol for Saturn*

Your Body: Understanding, Application & Practice

Your Blueprint: Mother, **Strength, Knowingness**

Nature: Moon

Practice: Sit quietly for some time each day in a state of complete quiet and stillness. Be aware of how you feel both emotionally and physically, what you think about, what you crave, what you are compelled to do. Track your discoveries in a journal.

Self Reflection: Do you use your intuition and ability to self-reflect in a way that evolves into wisdom, or do you linger in grandiosity or self-abasement? Do you take the time for self-reflection each day?

Wisdom

Experience

The divine is always in search of the many beings and creatures that walk the Earth to share its discoveries through their intentions and actions. The Sun holds and imparts cosmic wisdom as it shines down upon the earth, creating and destroying in a rhythmic and compassionate cycle of life. The human opens, and utilizes the energy to create its own wisdom through experience.

Sacred Body Wisdom

Sacred Symbolism: *Astrological Symbol for the Zodiac*

Your Body: Co-creation, Integration

Your Blueprint: Father, **Compassion, The Witness**

Nature: Sun

Practice: Know yourself. Begin to express and share your wisdom with those who can experience it with you. Be curious about life and others.

Self Reflection: Are you attached to the role of constant student or mentor to others? Are you ready to risk some of your entrenched habits to call-in people who can meet you where you are?

Windows to the Soul

Devotional Practices

Sincere attention and practice propel you through multiple and progressive windows of new opportunity, into the realms where you realize, and actualize, all things as spiritual in nature. Your body is glorified, spirit's communication is effortless—speaking through you from the god of your heart as the Wheel of Life turns in rhythm with the cycles of the universe.

Windows to the Soul is a series of cyclical and evolutionary practices that enhance awareness of your divinity in the body. They also balance the variances of energy in your personal planetary and elemental symbolism, your energy field, the subtle energy channels and centers. One by one, with devotion and commitment, you begin to acknowledge and strengthen the link between your physical and subtle forms, your soul's purpose and human experience, ultimately opening these windows and moving into your next step.

The Wheel of Life is your guide through each day and every season, the solar, lunar and breath cycles, your current life and the many other steps and milestones toward integration and limitless expansion. The Wheel of Life turns rhythmically and continuously throughout eternity, symbolizing all cycles.

Your Body
A practice, by its nature, engages the body: its physiology, emotions and mind. New activities create new neural networks and enhance your ability to dissolve old patterns.

Your Blueprint
These awareness practices encourage communication with your soul and other spiritual forces, helping you to integrate the energies from above and below.

Nature
Each practice encourages connections with bodily systems and functions through the elements. Breathing is air, visualization and awareness are ether, creative energy is water and fire,

movement is earth; inquiry, reflection, healing and mastery are fire.

Energetic Connections
Windows to the Soul is linked to all *Sacred Body Cards* and symbols. For more information, read about these *Sacred Gateways,* symbols and themes:

Triquetra—Unity
Vitruvian Man—Organic Body
Pentacle—The Elements
Rose—Sacred Cisterns
Sacred Spiral—Rivers and Streams
Flower of Life—Soul to Soul
Qabala—Mystical Journey
Triple Spiral—Gateways to the Heights

The Mystic's Journey
Many journeyers stop just before this gateway, going no further. Because you can see through the *Windows to the Soul,* you are capable of fooling yourself into believing you have passed through them. Do not allow resistance and unconsciousness—emotionally, mentally or physically, to stop your progress. The true *Sacred Gateway* is open only to those willing to embody the knowledge and entrain the body's evolution through dedication and sincere practice.

Breath of Life	Cultivating Creativity
Visualization	Awakening Awareness
Running Energy	Self-Inquiry & Reflection
Inner Rhythms	Self-Healing & Mastery

Sacred Body Wisdom

Your Map
There are 9 practical stepping-stones in *Windows to the Soul*, which resides in the 7th wisdom ring. Here you might just find your resistance.

Reflections
How do these activities assist you in your evolution? How do they reflect your relationship with self and others?

Conscious Breath	Currents & Tides	Movement
Touch	Inner Sight	The Aura
Sound	Sensing	Feeling
Action	Rhythm	Writing
Music & Art	Journaling	Vitality
Sexual Energies	Awareness of Awareness	

Self-Inquiry
Are you self-aware, or self-conscious? Do you acknowledge and accept your emotions and thoughts, or do you follow them, giving them too much energy and attention? Can you witness yourself, your creations and experiences with neutrality? Do you feel fluid with and connected to your natural rhythms; are you in resistance, or somehow find yourself pushing energy around?

Breath of Life

Gateway of Presence

Awakening: At birth or any beginning, you take your first breaths, anchoring spirit inside your body. As inspiration becomes you, stagnancy departs and vitality enters.

Sacred Body Wisdom

Sacred Symbolism: *Urquhart Castle, Loch Ness, Scotland*

Your Body: Heart, Lungs, Conscious Breath

Your Blueprint: Prana, **Tributaries**

Nature: Air, Wind, East, Vernal Equinox

Practice: Breathe consciously. The air moves through your nostrils, into your inner kingdom in the center of your head. Exhale any dross or unconsciousness. Do this each night before sleep and in the morning upon awakening.

Self Reflection: What are the similarities between the energies of breath, spring time, and new beginnings?

Visualization

Cauldron of Creativity

Creation: Every passing moment, every breath you take, is another opportunity to let go of the old and create something new.

Sacred Body Wisdom

Sacred Symbolism: *Window to the Sky, Ireland*

Your Body: Brain: Frontal Lobes, Awakening, Fertility

Your Blueprint: Energy Awareness, Sacred Marriage, **Envisioning, Clear Sight**

Nature: Southeast, Air & Fire

Practice: Visualize your next step and make a vision board. Focus on this board once daily for 21 days.

Self Reflection: Are you able to have what you create?

Running Energy

Gateway of Vitality

Transformation: Calling in the energies of Earth & Sky, you allow the great Mother and Father to awaken your body to its spiritual and soul forces.

Sacred Body Wisdom

Sacred Symbolism: *Abbey Ruins, Ireland*

Your Body: Definition, Expression, Health

Your Blueprint: Subtle Energy Channels; **Creative, Earth & Cosmic Energies**

Nature: Midsummer, South, Fire

Practice: Run Cosmic and Earth Energy through your body, into your auric field. Do this to clear and define your personal space.

Self Reflection: Are you willing to feel uncomfortable—experiencing the hurdles and deep resistance to your own stagnancy—so you can transform your cells for overall health and wellbeing?

Inner Rhythms

Cauldron of Affinity

Synchronicity: Galactic cycles create currents in the solar system; lunar cycles create planetary tides. Earth's tides and currents create the inner rhythms of your being and your relationship to your life as a spirit embodied.

Sacred Body Wisdom

Sacred Symbolism: *Celtic Cross in the Church Window, Ireland*

Your Body: Pineal Gland, Cerebellum, Movement, Dance, Song

Your Blueprint: Energy Circulation, **Balance**

Nature: Southwest, Fire & Water

Practice: Move with awareness, opening your joints and your primary energy centers. Do this to open the gateways so energy flows effortlessly through you.

Self Reflection: Are you willing to move slowly, thoughtfully, quietly and consciously? Are you wiling to do this enough so you can feel your inner rhythms?

Cultivating Creativity
Gateway of Expression

Devotion: Inspiration comes from within. There are three distinct sources of creativity in your 7 primary body chakras-procreativity, co-creativity and manifest creations. Express yourself!

Sacred Body Wisdom

Sacred Symbolism: *Three Church Windows, Ireland*

Your Body: Womb; Throat, Heart & Arms; Crown

Your Blueprint: 2nd, 4th & 5th, 7th Chakras, **Creative Energy**

Nature: Autumnal Equinox, West, **Water**

Practice: Become aware of your ability to birth new ways of being through co-creation and expression. Do this to express and manifest divinity in your body. Sing and dance your birth!

Self Reflection: How do you experience inspiration? How does it a-muse your creativity?

Self Inquiry & Reflection
Cauldron of Wisdom

Recapitulation: Your willingness to inquire within and self-reflect with honesty and sincerity is the first step in self-mastery. Your desire to simply reflect, rather than project, is the next step.

Sacred Body Wisdom

Sacred Symbolism: *Abbey Window, Lindisvarne, Scotland*

Your Body: Integration of all systems: physical, emotional, mental

Your Blueprint: All Energy Centers & Chakras, **Unity**

Nature: Northwest, **Water & Earth**

Practice: Spend time each evening reflecting on your day, making inquiries into your habits and fears. Do this to make room for your brilliance.

Self Reflection: Can you discern the difference between a reflection and a projection, whether it is yours going outward or someone else's coming toward you?

Awakening Awareness
Gateway of the Cosmos

Restoration: Self-awareness is human; awareness of awareness is divine. Call out the unconscious, bringing it into consciousness. Destroy what doesn't work and create awareness of your unconscious gifts.

Sacred Body Wisdom

Sacred Symbolism: *Window to the Sky, Irish Ruin*

Your Body: Self-Affinity, Focus, Awareness

Your Blueprint: Consciousness

Nature: Midwinter, North, Earth

Practice: Find a quiet, darkened space to gradually soften your senses. Lie down or sit in a comfortable chair. Close your eyes and use an eye cover if you like. Speak not a sound. Turn off the music, the phone, and any other devices. Be sure to handle any potential distractions and safety considerations before you go within. You might also consider any scents--try this practice without using anything aromatic. Breathe naturally and find comfort in this sense-free space. Be here for a while. Can you become aware of your awareness inside this stillness?

Self-Reflection: Do you enjoy being alone, or do you resist it? Do you like clutter or empty spaces? Can you be alone in an environment without sound or other media distractions? How long?

Self-Healing & Mastery
Cauldron of the Higher Self

Responsibility: Mastery emerges when you empower yourself to heal and make changes in your body-spirit framework. Healing the body is one thing; healing the blueprint is another.

Sacred Body Wisdom

Sacred Symbolism: *Church Ruins, Ireland*

Your Body: The Mind, Beliefs

Your Blueprint: Energy Mastery, **Unity**

Nature: Northeast, Earth & Air

Practice: Immediately shift your energy each time you begin to blame a person, place, or situation for your circumstances. Instead, plant the seeds of responsibility, watching the flowers grow.

Self-Reflection: Imagine you are the only person on earth—the creator of all. Are you willing to embrace that you are also fully capable of, and responsible for creating and healing yourself on every level? Can you take that sovereignty into your current life among so many others?

Gateways to the Heights
Spiritual Energy

Three distinctive portals open the "way-in" on your passage across the sea of consciousness. These entry points mark and hold the subtle fluid contents that crest and curl on your inner riverbeds. You readily surf the first two spirals of body and mind, yet the third wave of spirit will only carry you through this gateway once you've become a witness.

Sacred Body Wisdom

Gateways to the Heights guide you further inward to higher consciousness. See with your inner eye, the subtle energies running though the subtle channels of your esoteric anatomy. There are many gateways leading you to become more aware of the divine within, and the secret is found very close to home in your organic nature. The instructions are found in your subtle anatomy and related energies.

The **Triple Spiral** shows you the way from your home on the land (body), to the sea (mind-emotion), and then to the sky (spirit). When channeled appropriately and practiced with sincerity, the energies in the rivers and streams, both subtle and physical, have the potential to take you to the heavens, the under world, and your inner (middle) world. They connect you to the universal web, reminding you of who you really are. You are a hologram of the divine. Here you use your inherent psychic capacity to first open the gates, and then gracefully move through them.

Your Body
Breath (prana), and cerebral spinal fluid (chi or kundalini), are just two of the energies inherent to living beings that act as gateways to higher dimensions.

Your Blueprint
This theme expresses the subtlest forms of energy moving through your blueprint. When you experience or sense the subtle energy flows at this level, you are strengthening your light body.

Energetic Connections
Gateways to the Heights cards are linked to all themes and symbols.

Sacred Body Wisdom

For more information about their energetic connections, read about these *Sacred Gateways*, symbols and themes:

Triquetra—Unity
Vitruvian Man—Organic Body
Pentacle—The Elements
Rose—Sacred Cisterns
Sacred Spiral—Rivers & Streams
Flower of Life—Soul to Soul
Qabala—Mystical Journey
Wheel of Life—Windows to the Soul

The Mystic's Journey

The *Sacred Gateway* now opens through *Gateways to the Heights*. Not only awareness and practice, but also awareness of awareness—becoming conscious of your unconscious capabilities, is the key to finding your way back to Unity.

Body Currents   Earth & Cosmic Energies
Vortexes   Primordial Power
Life Forces   Divine Matrix
Creative Energy   Spiritual Essence

Your Map

On the final leg of your return journey home in the 8th ring of wisdom, you cross a series of 9 more *Stepping-Stones*, each representing a different subtle energy. Your consciousness is now becoming united with your spiritual energies because you have seen the channels. Your physical body begins to exist in a lighter form, your experiential consciousness has met and matched your spiritual awareness, and you are now working on your ascension body, one step away from the *Unity* gate.

Reflections
Your body is a sacred hologram for the divine. How do these energies guide your evolution; how do they reflect your relationship with your life as a spirit embodied?

Earth & Cosmic Energy	Ownership
Inspiration & Expiration	Creative Expression
Presence	Neutrality
Universal Connections	Spiritual Web or Matrix
Inner Voice	Essence Energy

Self-Inquiry
How present are you in any given moment? Do you occupy your body fully; who owns the air space immediately around you? Are you aware of the subtle energies moving through you? Are you connected to both earth and cosmos?

Body Currents

Nourishment

Blood, lymph, air, digestive fluids, hormones and other bio-chemicals are physical manifestations of your etheric body energies—also known as prana or chi. As you breathe, your etheric body breathes too, flowing through your blueprint, and informing the corresponding physical systems.

Sacred Body Wisdom

Sacred Symbolism: *Loch Awe, Scotland*

Your Body: Bodily Fluids, Circulatory and Detoxification Organs

Your Blueprint: Prana, Chi, Kundalini, Elemental & Magnetic Energies, **Vital Vessels**

Nature: Inland Channels & Seas

Practice: Find the center of your head. Look down to see your inner compass imprinted on your pelvic floor.

Self Reflection: Do you notice your bones—the hard outer coating and the softer center where the cells are actually born? Can you see from your mind's eye, the nerves and blood routes circulating throughout your body?

Earth & Cosmic Energies

Macrocosmic

Earth energy bubbles up from below, deep in the molten core of the planet, moving through your lower limbs. Cosmic energy beams down from beyond the Polestar, touching first your crown, and then every chakra on its way to find earth at your root. Together they circulate, defining you deep in the bones of your subtle anatomy.

Sacred Body Wisdom

Sacred Symbolism: *Ancient Archway, Iona, Scotland*

Your Body: Marrow, Fluids, Fascia

Your Blueprint: Sources, Subtle **Energy Channels**

Nature: Earth & Sky, Center of the Planet & the Galaxy

Practice: Center yourself. Place roses or other sacred symbols at the edge of your aura to represent all four directions.

Self Reflection: What if every cell in your body was a starry reflection of the cosmos, or the light reflected in a drop of water?

Vortexes

Anchoring Energies

Spinning wheels of light and vibration, this energy calls your attention into present time, clearing and centering. Linking your physical body to your subtle bodies and auric field, you take ownership of your personal space, and your certainty commands greater presence in daily life.

Sacred Body Wisdom

Sacred Symbolism: *Labyrinth, Santa Fe, New Mexico,*

Your Body: Joints, Nerve Plexi

Your Blueprint: Chakras, Anchor Points for the Subtle Bodies, **Anchorage**

Nature: Inner Tree Rings, Star Fish

Practice: From the center of your head, look down at your spine behind your navel, between and just below your kidneys. Envision a golden sun there; let it expand through the full depth of your body.

Self Reflection: Consider this: there are 7 nerve-blood plexi, 7 primary glands, and 7 body chakras, located in the same physical places. Do you see the overlay of your physical and subtle bodies? Can you feel the energy in your belly anchoring you in present time? Do you sense the anchor points in the tips of your finger and toes?

Primordial Power

Kundalini-Chi

Journeying deep into the wells of your center and your roots, you can feel the river of power rising within your core, up to the cosmic gateway at the crown of your head. This vital energy circulates in your brain and back down again through parallel sun and moon channels.

Sacred Body Wisdom

Sacred Symbolism: *Burial Chamber, Scotland*

Your Body: Cerebral Spinal Fluid

Your Blueprint: Golden Light, Kundalini, Chi, **The Riverbed**

Nature: The Light of Every Thing

Practice: Lay lengthwise on a foam or towel roll, supporting your head and tail at each end. Feel the weight of your head and sacrum. Breathe, watch and feel the golden light moving up and down your spine, allowing it to pool in your head and in your abdominal cauldron.

Self Reflection: Are you open to the possibility that cerebral spinal fluid is a hologram for kundalini or chi? How do you see it in your body, and how does it enhance your experience of spirit moving through you?

Life Forces

Pulse of Nature

Subtle, vital energies move through unseen channels from one inner island to the next. Much like the blood in your veins pulsing through and nourishing your vital organs, the energy in these streams feeds you for a more subtle awakening and transformation.

Sacred Body Wisdom

Sacred Symbolism: *Glencoe National Park, Scotland*

Your Body: Breath, Vibration

Your Blueprint: Prana, Apana, Chi, **Tributaries**

Nature: Glacial Valleys; Mountain Lakes, Rivers & Streams

Practice: Envision the glacier moving mountains, slowly creating valleys, lakes and streams. Now see the chi in your body in the same way, scouring away the stagnant energy.

Self Reflection: Can you envision your life forces pulsing through every cell and organ of your body, moving out stagnancy and filling them all with vitality?

Divine Matrix

Human Torus

Cultivate first, your own auric field. Become aware of how you create shared energy fields with other beings; how the universal tapestry is woven into all things. The energy around you is always in motion, reaching and connecting, blending and merging in a dance with all others.

Sacred Body Wisdom

Sacred Symbolism: *Abbey Ruins, Ireland*

Your Body: Cellular Matrix

Your Blueprint: Aura, **Streams**

Nature: Spider's Web, Natural Trellis'

Practice: See the river of energy fountaining up from your pelvic cauldron, through the centerline of your body, up and out through your crown chakra, down into your aura on all sides, under your feet, up through your legs and into your pelvis again. This is the eternal cycling of your personal energy.

Self Reflection: Can you picture the singularity of your own energy vibration and the way it emanates out from your body into the spaces around you? Can you see how it links to everything else?

Creative Energy

Wellsprings

Three wellsprings, three channels, all working synchronously to encourage your unique offering and the completion of your soul's mission. Blending divinity with your inherent ability to birth new ideas—creativity is sourced within, and expressed through choice and action.

Sacred Body Wisdom

Sacred Symbolism: *Dolmen Quoit, Cornwall, England*

Your Body: Sexual Energy, Vibration

Your Blueprint: 2nd, 5th, 7th Chakras, **Wellsprings**

Nature: Caves, Ancient Burial & Ceremonial Chambers

Practice: A spring of color fountains up from your pelvis into your throat. A beam of light shines down from the cosmos into your head and then meets the fountain in your throat. Watch as this mixture of brilliance moves into your arms and fountains out your hands.

Self Reflection: Are you aware of the qualities of the three creative centers of your blueprint: procreation, expression & co-creation? Are you able to see your creativity moving through your arms and hands, out into the world?

Spiritual Essence

Human Divinity

A brilliant combination of vitality, divinity and soul, your spiritual essence is the highest possible body frequency. Its brilliant droplets shower down from your crown, opening your body to spirit, imprinting the wisdom reminiscent of your origins. Your past and future merge into time out of time with the energy of your spiritual essence.

Sacred Body Wisdom

Sacred Symbolism: *Celtic Cross, Ireland*

Your Body: Pineal & Pituitary Glands, Thalamus, Hypothalamus

Your Blueprint: The Inner Kingdom, **Pools of Energy**

Nature: Center of the Milky Way Galaxy

Practice: Draw your attention into the center of your head. Look up to see a halo of light hovering over you. Watch as a golden sun is birthed from inside the halo. Fill that sun with your highest creative potential and watch as its energy flows down through your head, filling your body and your aura.

Self Reflection: What if the Christ in you was waiting to be remembered?

"The Sacred Body Cards are refreshingly new and different! Exquisite Celtic designs accompany photographic images from Ireland & Britain that create a profound perspective on the wisdom of the human body and its relationship with all that is. A multi-dimensional wisdom is embedded in this unique deck.'"

MK- England

Michele Geyer is the creator of the *Sacred Body Oracle and Cards* and the author of "Sacred Body Wisdom: *Mystical Conversations* Between Body & Spirit;" the upcoming *"Relax your Body, Quiet your Mind: 52 Ways to Relieve Stress,"* and *"Sacred Body Calendar Journal."*

All photos for the *Sacred Body Oracle Card* images were taken during personal journeys while working and traveling on location in Ireland, England, Scotland, and the Highlands Wildlife Preserve, the Pacific Northwest, the California Coastal Redwoods,

Northern New Mexico, the Atlanta Aquarium, and Northern California.

Currently living in The Pacific Northwest, her soul home is still in Ireland.

Connect with Michele directly for a *Sacred Body Oracle Session*, correspondence courses, tele-seminars and in-person programs: *Creating Clarity, Sacred Body Wellness, and Walking the Evolutionary Path*.

Contact Michele: sacredbodypathworking.com/contact.html

References

Design & Recording:
Lucid Design Studios: luciddesignstudios.com

Earth-Based Studies:
Lunaea Weatherstone: lunaea.com
Mara Freeman's Chalice Center: chalicecentre.net
Order of Bards, Ovates & Druids: druidry.org
Santa Fe Shamanic Healing: luisakolker.com

Intuitive Training:
Clairvoyant Hawaii: clairvoyanthawaii.com
Magic Isle: magicisle.com

Pilates:
Inner Rhythms Pilates: innerrhythmspilates.com

Sacred Body Wisdom:
Sacred Body Oracle & Cards: sacredbodyoracleandcards.com
Sacred Body Oracle and Cards Companion Books:
"Sacred Body Pathworking: An Evolutionary Journey"
"Relax Your Body, Quiet Your Mind:
52 Ways to Relieve Stress & Go Within"
"Sacred Body Wisdom:
Mystical Conversations Between Body & Spirit"

Workshops & Courses:
Awakening the Mystical Conversation Between Body & Spirit:
sacredbodypathworking.com

www.ingramcontent.com/pod-product-compliance
Lightning Source LLC
Chambersburg PA
CBHW070548010526
44118CB00012B/1266